W9-BRA-117

on being
PENTECOSTAL

on being
PENTECOSTAL

DAVID K. BERNARD
ROBIN JOHNSTON

On Being Pentecostal

David K. Bernard
Robin Johnston

Cover Design by Abraham LaVoi
Interior Page Design by Laura Jurek

Printed in United States of America

WORD AFLAME PRESS
8855 Dunn Road, Hazelwood, MO 63042
www.pentecostalpublishing.com

Library of Congress Cataloging-in-Publication Data

Bernard, David K., 1956-
    On being Pentecostal / by David K. Bernard and Robin M. Johnston.
        p. cm.
    ISBN 978-1-56722-951-6
    1. Pentecostalism. I. Johnston, Robin M., 1957- II. Title.
    BR1644.B47 2011
    230'.046--dc23

                        2011034345

Table of Contents

Introduction

For some people "Pentecostal" is a new word. A century ago it was rarely part of the average North American's vocabulary. However, its use has risen steadily, most often in reference to the fastest-growing segment of the Christian faith. Although it has become much more common in recent years, it is not a new word. Its roots go back to an ancient Jewish feast that celebrated the first fruits of the harvest. The Hebrews of antiquity were primarily an agrarian society and a successful harvest was critical to their wellbeing. They celebrated God's blessing and provision for them with a feast, which fell on the fiftieth day after another important feast day, the Passover, hence its moniker. But for Christians, Pentecost takes on a different meaning. It marks the birthday of the church.

The Bible records the first outpouring of the Holy Spirit on the earliest believers on the Day of Pentecost. Per the instructions given to them by Jesus just before His ascension, the disciples—or followers of Jesus—gathered in Jerusalem to await the outpouring of the Spirit. Early on the morning of the Day of Pentecost, the Spirit fell upon 120 believers. The excitement of this experience spread throughout the crowds gathered from around the Mediterranean in Jerusalem for the Feast of Pentecost. (See Acts 2.) They were particularly intrigued by the ecstatic behavior and multiple languages spoken by those newly filled with the Spirit. When a curious crowd had assembled around the meeting place of the believers, Peter addressed the gathering to explain the experiences and actions of what would become known as the church.

These events took place shortly after the crucifixion and resurrection of Jesus Christ. Not only were the disciples attempting to understand the significance of the crucifixion and resurrection, but the broader Jewish population was also struggling to understand them. Peter associated the experiences of Pentecost with a prophecy given hundreds of years prior by the Hebrew prophet Joel. Peter reminded the crowd "this was that spoken by Joel." This was the prophesied outpouring of the Spirit and it was for everybody. A significant portion of the crowd responded to Peter's preaching and the church began to rapidly expand.

The Book of Acts records the experiences and teachings of this new movement. Because many of the key players of the Acts church were eyewitnesses to the life and teachings of Jesus, it follows that they would have the clearest insight into the way in which to worship Jesus. As a result the church in Acts should function as a model to follow when attempting to build a church. However, over the centuries the institutional church lost sight of the Acts pattern. Just over a hundred years ago, a rising interest in the restoration of the Acts or apostolic church birthed the modern Pentecostal movement.

This short volume will serve as an introduction to Pentecostalism. It is divided into three parts. Part I covers four key doctrines of the movement. Part II introduces four distinctive practices. And in Part III, the authors attempt to share a brief history of the Pentecostal movement and to tell a number of stories of individual Pentecostals. Take a few moments of your time to learn what it means to be Pentecostal.

...blish the land,

...to the people,

...rtion the desolate heritages,

...the prisoners, 'Come out,'

...who are in darkness, 'Appear.'

...feed along the ways,

...e heights shall be their

...r,

...hunger or thirst,

...hing wind nor sun shall

...n,

...ty on them will lead

...water will guide

...mountains a

...ll be raised up,

...from afar,

...he north and

...Syene.·

...ult.

places

and your devastated land—

surely now you will be too narrow for

your inhabitants,

and those who swallowed you up will

be far away.

20 The children of your bereavement

will yet say in your ears:

'The place is too narrow for me;

make room for me to dwell in.'

21 Then you will say in your heart:

'Who has borne me these?

I was bereaved and barren,

exiled and put away,

but who has brought up these?

Behold, I was left alone;

from where have these come?' "

22 Thus says the Lord GOD:

"Behold, I will lift up my hand to the

nations,

and raise my signal to the peoples;

and they shall bring your sons in their

bosom,

and your daughters shall be carried on

their shoulders.

23 Kings shall be your foster fathers,

and their queens your nursing mothers.

...e and your desolate

bride.

...that I am the LORD your Savior,

and your Redeemer, the Mighty One

of Jacob."

Israel's Sin and the Servant's Obedience

50 Thus says the LORD:

"Where is your mother's certificate

of divorce,

with which I sent her away?

Or which of my creditors is it

to whom I have sold you?

Behold, for your iniquities you were

sold,

and for your transgressions your

mother was sent away.

2 Why, when I came, was there no man;

why, when I called, was there

to answer?

Is my hand shortened, th... it cannot

redeem?

Or have I no po... to deliver?

Behold, by my ...uke I dry ...

I make the ...

their fish st... ...rs a dese...

and die ...thirst.

3 I clothe the ...

and ...

4 The L... GOD ha... ...blackness

the tongue of those ...are taught,

that I may know how to ...tain with a

word

him who is weary.

Morning by morning he a...

he awakens my ear

to hear as those who are ...ht.

*Dead Sea Scroll, Syriac, Vulgate (see also verse 25); Masoretic Text of a righteous man

wine,

...know

...tr

11 Be...

This yo...

you ...

Lord's Co...

51 "Liste...

right...

you who...

look to the ...

hewn...

and to the ...

were d...

2 Look to Abra...

and to Sarah ...

for he was but ...

that I might b...

him.

3 For the LORD co...

he comforts all ...

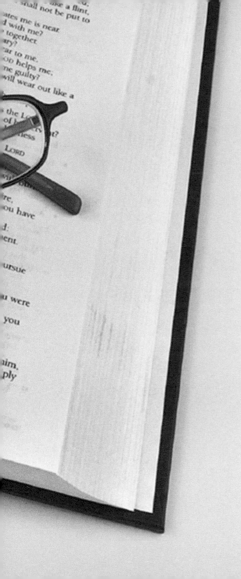

Part I

Our Beliefs

Our Very Present Help: God with Us

"Jesus Christ is the same yesterday, and today, and forever"
(Hebrews 13:9).

Eighteenth-century Christian philosopher William Paley was a leading proponent of natural theology. He is best known for his watchmaker analogy in which he compared a watch found on the side of the road to the physical world. Paley insisted that no one would doubt the watch had a maker. He then argued that the world is much more complex and therefore must have a designer. Paley understood that designer to be God. He went on to suggest that the way we gain insight into this God is by studying the world He designed. This is sometimes called natural theology.

While there is merit to Paley's reasoning, God is more than the world's designer; He is intimately involved in the world daily. He is not like an absentee landlord, distant and unapproachable, rather as the writer of Hebrews stated, He is "touched with the feeling of our infirmities" (Hebrews 4:15). He is our very present help—that friend who sticks closer than a brother. He is actively engaged not only in the world at large but also in the life of an individual believer. We can encounter Him in a number of avenues.

Revelation

Artist and author Martin Handford created a cultural phenomenon when he released the first *Where's Waldo* book. Waldo, a toque-wearing, bespectacled, cartoon character, was cleverly hidden on each page of the book and the reader was challenged to find him. Although the instructions are simple, the task is much more difficult. It is easy to fritter hours away trying to find Waldo and still be unable to locate him on every page.

It is easier to find God than it is to find Waldo. In Acts 17, Paul reminded the crowd gathered on Mars Hill in Athens that, if we seek Him, God "is not far from each one of us" (Acts 17:27). The primary revelation of God was the person of Jesus Christ. Two thousand years ago God became flesh and lived among us. He was born in the Judean village of Bethlehem, grew up in Nazareth of Galilee, and at thirty years of age began teaching and performing miracles. His earthly life was cut short by a crucifixion, but after three days He arose from the grave and shortly thereafter ascended into Heaven. In I

Corinthians 15 Paul grounded our hope of eternal life in the experience of Jesus Christ. His resurrection gave proof to the hope of our resurrection and His death in our stead provided the covering of our sin so we could eternally dwell in His presence.

The primary knowledge of the person of Jesus Christ comes to us from the Bible. In addition to the Gospel accounts, the Bible provides key insights into the nature of God. The Bible is written revelation inspired by God. It follows then that through its pages we can begin to learn what God is like, how we should please Him, and some idea of how we can expect Him to interact with us.

The Bible is more than an inspired account of history past. It is the living Word. "For the word of God is living and powerful, and sharper than any two-edged sword, piercing even to the division of soul and spirit, and of joints and marrow, and is a discerner of the thoughts and intents of the heart (Hebrews 4:12). One way to encounter God is through His Word. We both learn about God and encounter Him via His Word.

As alluded to in the introduction of this chapter, God reveals Himself to us in nature. The Psalmist declared, "The heavens declare the glory of God; and the firmament shows His handiwork (Psalm 19:1). You gain insight into an artist by studying his work. You know something about a carpenter by examining his craftsmanship. When you watch the sun slip over the horizon you can reasonably conclude that God has an appreciation for beauty.

However, we must never forget that we live in a fallen world. Sin continues to etch an ugly pattern on our surroundings. Sin in this context is not necessarily referring to individual sin but rather to the effects of the Fall on life as we know it. In addition to beautiful sunsets, nature also provides destructive tornados. Sometimes these disasters are even pejoratively referred to as "acts of God," which perhaps gives more insight into the speaker than God. We can learn about God through nature but we rarely encounter Him there.

God also reveals Himself through personal encounter. The Bible is filled with stories of God interacting with humankind. He gave Noah plans for an ark; He tested Abraham's faith on Mount Moriah; He wrestled with Jacob beside a brook. Sometimes the encounters were more ethereal. Paul was caught up to the third heaven and John was in the Spirit on the Lord's Day. Sometimes God speaks through another person or an angel. The prophet Nathan rebuked David's sin. An angel visited Joseph to share with him the unbelievable events occurring in the life of his beloved Mary.

It follows that if God is unchangeable, then not only did He interact with Bible characters but He also continues to encounter people today. The Book of Acts does not contain a formal conclusion. It just stops. Perhaps Luke broke off the narrative in the way he did as an encouragement for readers to write themselves into the story. God was active in Acts. His active engagement, primarily as the Holy Spirit, energized the church. We should anticipate that same active engagement in the church today.

The Indwelling Spirit

Chapter 4 will discuss the "new birth"—a birth of water and Spirit. The Holy Spirit not only regenerates new believers, but He also is actively involved in the ongoing life of a believer. Paul encouraged the Galatian church to walk in the Spirit (Galatians 5:25). Jesus promised His disciples that after His bodily ascension the Comforter would come and He would lead and guide them into all truth (John 14:26).

Both Jesus and Paul expected an ongoing encounter between a believer and the Holy Spirit. In Ephesians Paul contrasted being drunk with wine and being filled with the Spirit. (See Ephesians 5:18.) Intoxicating drink alters the thoughts and actions of the person under its influence. So too should the indwelling Spirit.

The Bible does not speak of the Spirit as an impersonal force. Rather it presents the Holy Spirit as God Himself. And while the initial baptism or infilling of a believer by the Spirit is experienced in time and space, it is the ongoing relationship between the believer and the Spirit that is the focus of the New Testament church. Although we are invited into a relationship with God we must always be aware of the unequal nature of this relationship. He is God and we are not. Our knowledge of Him is limited by the restrictions of our humanity. The language the Bible uses to help us pursue a relationship with the Spirit illustrates this reality. We are to be baptized with the Spirit—which implies we are to be immersed in the Spirit. On the other hand, we are to be filled with the Spirit implying that He will live in us. This is not to suggest the Bible has contradictory messages, rather it illustrates the "otherness" of God and our human limitations. Like all relationships, this relationship is better experienced than analyzed.

Miracles

One of the ways in which God is "other" is that He is supernatural. He possesses power beyond the natural world and has the ability to suspend the laws of nature. We usually refer to this activity as a miracle.

The word "miracle" has become overused. An unlikely comeback in the ninth inning of a ballgame is called a miracle comeback. A skillful surgeon performing a delicate operation is sometimes referred to as a miracle worker. While the dictionary may recognize this secondary use of the word, biblical miracles were supernatural events. Water was turned to wine. Blind eyes were opened—and not by skillful surgeons. The lame did walk. Five thousand were fed with five loaves and two fish blessed by Jesus. Similar miracles are recorded in the Book of Acts. The apostles, when first faced with persecution, were undaunted: "Now, Lord, look on their threats, and grant to Your servants that with all boldness they may speak Your word, by stretching out Your hand to heal, and that signs and wonders may be done through the name of Your holy Servant Jesus" (Acts 4:29-30). Paul was instrumental in raising a person from the dead and casting out evil spirits. (See Acts 16:16-19; 20:9-11.) Since the Bible nowhere records that these were special events for a limited time, we should expect similar experiences today.

The Bible outlines four elements that contribute to miracles and healings. Faith is the first element. Even a cursory reading of the Gospels reveals that faith is critical in the working of miracles. Perhaps Matthew best illustrates this when he contrasts the "no" faith of the religious leaders, the "little" faith of the disciples, and the "great" faith of a few outsiders such as the Syrophoenician woman (Matthew 15:22-28). Her great faith impressed Jesus and her daughter was delivered. Although we must be careful not to surmise that a faith formula can be developed—after all He is God and we are not—faith in His ability contributes to miracles.

The second element associated with New Testament miracles is the name of Jesus. In Acts, the apostles consistently invoked the name of Jesus when expecting a miracle. A link exists between the name of Jesus and the release of His power. To pray or baptize in the name of Jesus is to recognize His authority. It shows an understanding of the covenant relationship between Him and us.

The Book of James outlines a third element linked with miracles and in particular with healing. "Is anyone among you sick? Let him call for the elders of the church, and let them pray over him, anointing him with oil in the name of the Lord. And the prayer of faith will save the sick, and the Lord will raise him up. And if he has committed sins, he will be forgiven" (James 5:14-15). God often mediates His power through humans. He works in community with the church. The "laying on of hands" is one way God shows His willingness to build up a community of believers.

The fourth element grows out of the atonement provided by substitionary death of Jesus Christ. "But He was wounded for our transgressions, He was bruised for our iniquities; the chastisement for our peace was upon Him, and by His stripes we are healed (Isaiah 53:5). The death, burial, and resurrection of Jesus Christ made eternal life possible for believers. He purchased us with His blood (Acts 20:28). When time is fulfilled we will witness the full impact of this atonement. Until then, we can expect moments when the end of time breaks in on the present and bodies are healed and miracles are wrought. He is our very present help.

The modern Pentecostal movement was birthed in an atmosphere of miracles. People were often initially drawn to the movement because they needed a healing or another type of miracle. One of the earmarks of Pentecostalism is the baptism of the Holy Spirit, which is a supernatural phenomenon. When people receive the Spirit they speak in other tongues—that is, in an unlearned language. This ecstatic speech is sometimes known as glossolalia. The New Testament presents tongues as both an initial and an ongoing experience in the life of a believer. It is the initial physical evidence of Spirit baptism and also it functions as a way to edify or build up a believer (I Corinthian 14:4).

The God presented in the New Testament was more than a teacher of morality. He was more than a dispenser of decrees. He was intimately involved in the life of believers, in the person of Jesus Christ and in the outpouring of His Spirit. And while He is not physically present with us today, His Spirit abides within the hearts of believers. He is our very present help. You can expect to encounter Him, perhaps today. He can become your very present help.

CHAPTER 2

The Revelation of God: The Bible

P entecostals believe it is important to be led of the Spirit. When His disciples were in despair because Jesus announced His impending departure from this world, He promised He would send the Spirit of truth who would guide them into all truth. (See John 16:13.) However, this desire to be led of the Spirit does not conflict with a high view of the Bible as a primary source for truth. We worship Him in Spirit and in truth.

If we believe in God, we should also believe in the Word of God. Since God was interested enough to create us, and since He created us as rational be-ings, surely He is interested enough to communicate with us and thereby fulfill His purpose for creation. All intelligent beings seek to communicate, and the Supreme Intelligence is no exception.

Since God is the Father of the human race, surely He wishes to have a relationship with His children. Since He loves us enough to impart life to us and sustain us, surely He desires to communicate His love to us and help us. From our belief in an intelligent, loving Creator, we should expect to find the Word of God among us. We would expect God to reveal His message in writing, the historic medium best suited for precision, preservation, and propagation.

The Bible Is God's Word

How can we know what is God's Word? We would expect God's Word to identify itself clearly and convincingly, to tell the truth about the human condition, to contain content worthy of its Author, and to address our deepest spiritual needs. When we examine the world's literature, it is evident that the Bible is the unique written Word of God to humanity. It is the first and foremost book to tell us the fundamental truth about our lives: all have sinned and need a Savior. The Bible bids us to investigate the truth for ourselves. "Test all things; hold fast what is good" (I Thessalonians 5:21). It also admonishes us to be prepared to explain the basis of our faith to others (I Peter 3:15).

The Bible asserts its unique status as the Word of God, and it speaks with self-vindicating authority. The prophets and apostles who wrote the Bible testified that the Spirit of God moved upon them as they wrote. Jesus Christ endorsed the Old Testament as Scripture, and He commissioned the writers of the New Testament to proclaim His message. Thus, if we accept Jesus Christ as Lord, we will accept the authority of the Bible.

We can establish that the Bible is God's Word by carefully examining its claims, character, historical and scientific verification, and impact upon human society. The fulfilled prophecies of the Scriptures are an amazing testimony to its divine origin. Finally, we can demonstrate the truth of the Bible by applying it to our lives, receiving its promises, and experiencing its dynamic power personally.

The cumulative effect of these points is to establish overwhelmingly, beyond reasonable doubt, that the Bible is God's revelation to us. God has challenged us to prove His Word; when we do we will find it to be true in every way. The Bible then becomes the standard of truth by which we measure all things.

The Inspiration of the Bible

The ultimate author of the Bible is God Himself. "All Scripture is given by inspiration of God, and is profitable for doctrine, for reproof, for correction, for instruction in righteousness" (II Timothy 3:16). "Inspiration" literally means "God-breathed." The picture is one of God breathing out words from His mouth (Matthew 4:4), creating Scripture similar to the way He created the universe (Psalm 33:6). In other words, the Bible emanated from God. It is God's communication to humanity. Inspiration here means more than the general creative impulse that prompts poets and musicians; it refers to action by God.

It means the work of the Holy Spirit upon divinely chosen authors whereby specific writings are trustworthy and authoritative.

Strictly speaking, inspiration refers to the original writing process and text; that is, the Bible does not say all subsequent efforts to copy and translate Scripture would be inspired. To the extent that there are deficiencies of textual transmission and translation, we cannot attribute them to God's inspiration. As we will discuss, we can have great confidence in the text we have today and affirm it as God's revelation to us.

The inspiration of Scripture extends to every word. Jesus said, "Man shall not live by bread alone, but by every word that proceeds from the mouth of God" (Matthew 4:4). Small phrases of Scripture, historical details, grammatical forms, individual words, and even individual letters all have significance. God warned, "Do not diminish a word" (Jeremiah 26:2). Jesus said, "Till heaven and earth pass away, one jot or one tittle will by no means pass from the law till all is fulfilled" (Matthew 5:18). Inspiration extends to all parts of the Bible; the Bible is fully and completely God's Word. (See Romans 15:4; II Peter 1:20-21.)

While the Bible is God's Word, it was also written by humans so that it is a divine-human work. God directly dictated some passages, such as the Ten Commandments, but from the different styles of writing we see that the background of the various biblical writers influenced their manner of expression. God chose and prepared writers suited to His purpose and used their individual characteristics. While the human writers employed words that reflected their language, culture, personality, education, experiences, and circumstances, God guided the process so that each word would accurately convey His message. The vocabulary is the writers', but the message is God's.

The Authority of the Bible

The Bible is God's authoritative revelation to us. It imparts saving knowledge, teaches, rebukes, corrects, trains, and equips; and as such it is our authority for salvation, Christian life, Christian ministry, and sound doctrine (II Timothy 3:15-17; 4:2-4). It is our teacher and guide (Psalm 119:11, 104-5).

Salvation comes by obeying God's Word (Roman 6:17-18; I Peter 1:22-25). If we do not believe, obey, and love God's Word, we will be lost (II Thessalonians 1:8; 2:9-15). We must let the Bible mold our worldview, our purpose in life, and our way of life. Our response to its message will determine our eternal destiny.

The Truthfulness of the Bible

Since the Bible is the Word of God, the Bible is truth. (See Psalm 119:89, 160; Proverbs 30:5; Romans 3:4.) It is infallible and inerrant—a reliable, trustworthy guide in all matters; free from falsehood, mistake, or failure; neither misleading nor misled; entirely true in everything it teaches. Just as Jesus is God manifested in human flesh yet without sin, so the Bible is God's Word communicated through humans yet without error.

We cannot hold ancient writers to our notions and conventions, however. Instead, we must read the Scriptures according to the customs, standards, and modes of understanding of their times. The inerrancy of Scripture allows for (1) the recording of false statements and sinful actions by Bible characters; (2) illustrations, figures of speech, and literary devices, including parables, poetry, similes, and metaphors; (3) quotations from nonbiblical sources; (4) use of nonscientific, phenomenal, or culturally relative speech; (5) different personalities, styles, and modes of expression; (6) adaptation to the limitations of human thinking; (7) general statements or accounts, including indirect dialogue, summaries, and stylized presentations; and (8) errors of transmission, which scholars seek to eliminate through a study and comparison of ancient manuscripts.

We should also consider the following points when we encounter difficulties or seeming discrepancies: (1) The Bible does not always say everything on a subject at once. (2) Not everything in the Bible is immediately clear to us, because of our distance from the original situation. (3) The Bible sometimes describes similar but different events or the same events from different points of view. (4) The Bible does not speak in the language of secular science and history or give full knowledge in these areas. (5) Errors can exist in our understanding of these matters or in our interpretation of Scripture.

The Canon

The canon is the list of books accepted as Scripture. God established the canon by inspiring certain books. God's people do not create the canon but discover and acknowledge it. When a book of the Bible was originally written,

God's people in that generation recognized it as inspired of God primarily on the basis of authorship and content. Subsequent generations also looked at the history of its reception by the people of God.

Since God desired to communicate His Word to us, we can be confident that He not only inspired it initially but also ensured that we would be able to recognize it. Otherwise, His purpose for inspiring the Bible would be thwarted. Therefore, we understand the historical recognition of the canon as a providential process guided by the Holy Spirit.

For the Old Testament, prophets apparently kept a register of prophetic writings and added to the collection as God inspired them. God's people, in turn, recognized this ongoing process. According to Jewish tradition, Ezra and Nehemiah collected the inspired books. The Old Testament canon was probably complete by about 400 BC. The Jews, God's chosen people under the old covenant, recognized the books of the Old Testament as God's Word and transmitted them to us. Jesus and the apostles accepted the Old Testament as the Word of God.

For the New Testament, the primary test of the canon is apostolic authority. Of the nine authors, five were recognized as apostles, in the sense that they were eyewitnesses of Jesus and founding leaders of the first-century church. These five are Matthew, John, Peter, Paul, and James, and they account for twenty-two of the books. For the remaining books, the authors (Mark, Luke, Jude, and author of Hebrews) were closely associated with the apostles.

The apostles and their associates were uniquely qualified to write the New Testament as eyewitnesses of Jesus (John 15:27; Acts 1:21-22). He called them personally and commissioned them to preach, teach, and make disciples (Matthew 28:19-20; John 17:17-20). Although Paul came later, he had a personal, supernatural encounter with Jesus Christ and received from Him an apostolic commission that the other apostles recognized. Since their day, no one has the qualifications to add to Scripture or proclaim another message. (See Galatians 1:8-9; Ephesians 2:20; Revelation 21:14; 22:18-19.)

The early church accepted the apostolic writings as inspired shortly after they were written. (See I Timothy 5:18, quoting Luke 10:7; II Peter 3:15-16.) The New Testament itself contains evidence of the reading, circulation, and collection of inspired writings. By about AD 150 we find in Christian writings numerous quotations representing every New Testament book except one to four short personal letters. By about AD 200 we have clear postbiblical witnesses to every book of the New Testament.

Ultimately, we accept the biblical canon by faith, based on the lordship of Jesus Christ. When we study this unique Book, hear its voice of authority, and trace its providential history, the Spirit bears witness with our spirit that its sixty-six books are the Word of God.

The Text of the Bible

No book from the ancient world comes to us with more integrity than the Bible. The authenticity of the Old Testament text is upheld by the high quality of the transmission process (the extreme care taken by the Jewish scribes) and has been vindicated by the Dead Sea Scrolls. The authenticity of the New

Testament text is upheld by the large quantity of manuscripts, which tend to cancel out errors, and the relatively short time lapse between the originals and the oldest existing copies.

Based on God's promises and His reasons for inspiring Scripture, we can trust the text transmitted to us. By faith and on the evidence, we can affirm that God has so protected His Word from doctrinal error that, despite the lengthy transmission process, our Bible proclaims all essential truths and contains nothing contrary to those truths. Otherwise, it would seem that sinful humans have thwarted God's plan in giving us the Bible.

Although there are differing readings among manuscripts and different approaches to resolving them, in the final analysis these textual variations have no doctrinal significance and do not diminish our trust in God's Word. From a study and comparison of the ancient manuscripts, it is apparent that God has indeed preserved His Word to all generations. (See Psalm 100:5; 105:8.) In His providence He has ensured that any scribal errors or changes would not become widely accepted or, if accepted, would still harmonize with the message of His eternal Word. As a result, the Bible we have today is effective in our lives as the Word of God.

Translations of the Bible

The Bible was originally written in Hebrew, Aramaic, and Greek. If we cannot read these languages, we should select relatively literal translations for primary reading and study, for two reasons. First, the nature of inspiration means that each word of Scripture is significant, not merely the general ideas. Second, the authoritative nature of Scripture and the purposes for which God gave it indicate that we need to study its meaning carefully and not merely be content with a general understanding. A literal translation attempts as much as possible to translate word for word but not so rigidly that it violates normal English usage. The classic literal translation in English is the King James Version (1611). Because of significant changes in word meaning and use over the centuries, readers of the KJV need the assistance of dictionaries and word studies. The New King James Version, the New American Standard Bible, and the English Standard Version are good literal translations in contemporary English.

Another type of translation is the dynamic equivalence. It seeks to translate thought for thought or phrase for phrase in order to produce a similar effect on the modern reader as the original text had on the ancient reader. The New International Version and New Living Translation are good dynamic-equivalent translations by conservative scholars that seek to be faithful to the inspired text while providing a more idiomatic rendition for modern readers. For thorough study, it is good to use both types of translations.

Paraphrases, such as The Living Bible and The Message, are restatements in different words that attempt to clarify the meaning of Scripture. They can serve as introductions or commentaries, but we should not equate them with Scripture itself.

Conclusion

The Bible admonishes us to be diligent to receive the approval of God, thereby avoiding shame (II Timothy 2:15). We do so by "rightly dividing," or correctly handling, the word of truth as a skilled worker. If we expect to receive God's approval we must read, study, interpret, preach, and teach the Bible in a careful, thorough, and correct manner. In order to benefit from the Bible, not only must we read and study it but we must believe and obey it.

"The Word of God is living and powerful" (Hebrews 4:12). The words of Jesus are spirit and life (John 6:63). When we read, study, and listen to the Bible, we hear the voice of the living Lord speaking to us today. We receive the message that can transform our lives and lead to us eternal life.

For Further Study

Bernard, David K. *God's Infallible Word*. Hazelwood, MO: Word Aflame Press, 1992.

Bernard, David K. *Understanding God's Word*. Hazelwood, MO: Word Aflame Press, 2005.

The Mighty God in Christ

The first verse of the Bible introduces God as the Creator of the universe. The Bible does not try to prove that God exists; it assumes His existence as fundamental. Creation itself bears witness that there is an intelligent, omnipotent, loving Creator (Romans 1:20). As we will discuss, the Bible teaches that there is one God. He is a personal being, not an abstract substance that contains a plurality of persons. The Bible further teaches that Jesus Christ is the one God manifested in the flesh. In Jesus dwells all the fullness of the Godhead bodily.

The Existence of God

There can be only one of three explanations for the existence of the universe: (1) it has always existed (eternal universe); (2) it came into existence by its own power (self-creating universe), or (3) God created it. Accepting any of these requires a faith that transcends scientific proof. It is more plausible to believe in an intelligent, eternal, omnipotent Creator than in the eternity or self-creative ability of nonrational matter.

The orderliness and design of the universe require the existence of a Designer. The incredible complexity of even the simplest forms of life shows that life did not begin by accident or blind chance. The moral nature of humanity reveals that we are more than intelligent animals; we were created in the image of a rational, spiritual, moral Being. Every human child develops a conscience, and every human society has a sense of morality (Romans 2:15).

How could the finite human mind even conceive of an infinite and perfect God unless God imparted that concept? Every society in history has expressed belief in a Supreme Being, and anthropological studies show that the most fundamental religious concept is not belief in many gods but belief in a supreme God. The testimony of the Scriptures and the confirmation of personal experience assure us that God indeed lives and communicates with humanity. Ultimately, we accept the truth of His existence by faith (Hebrews 11:6).

The Nature of God

"God is Spirit" (John 4:24). He is not made of flesh, blood, bones, or physical matter. He is invisible to the human eye unless He chooses to reveal Himself in some way (John 1:18). God has individuality, rationality, and personality. He is self-existent, eternal, and unchanging. He is omnipresent (everywhere present), omniscient (all knowing and all wise), and omnipotent (all powerful). (See Psalm 139.)

God's moral nature includes holiness, justice and righteousness, mercy and grace, love, faithfulness, truth, and goodness. He is absolutely perfect in every way. I John 4:8 says, "God is love"; no other religion identifies God so totally with love.

The Oneness of God

God is absolutely and indivisibly one. "Hear, O Israel: The LORD our God, the LORD is one!" (Deuteronomy 6:4). He is the First and the Last; there is no God beside Him; He created everything alone and by Himself; and He is the only Savior (Isaiah 44:6, 8, 24; 45:21-23). Many other passages emphasize God's oneness. (See Isaiah 42:8; 43:10-11; 46:6-9; Mark 12:28-30; Galatians 3:20; I Timothy 2:5; James 2:19.) Consequently, there are no distinctions in God's eternal being; the Godhead does not consist of plural centers of consciousness. All names and titles of the Deity refer to one and the same being.

God has revealed Himself as Father, in the Son, and as the Holy Spirit. These roles are necessary to God's plan of redemption for fallen humanity. In order to save us, God provided a sinless Man to die in our place—the Son, in whose name we receive salvation (John 20:31). In foreordaining the plan of salvation and begetting the Son, God is the Father. In working to transform and empower us, applying salvation to us individually, God is the Holy Spirit. In sum, these titles describe God's redemptive works but do not indicate three eternal persons, just as the Incarnation does not indicate that God had eternally preexistent flesh.

The title of Father describes God as father of all creation and more specifically of His people (Deuteronomy 32:6; Malachi 2:10). In the New Testament, God is the Father of the Son. The title of Son refers to God coming in the flesh, for the child Jesus was begotten miraculously by God's Spirit and thus was actually the Son of God (Luke 1:35). The title of Holy Spirit describes God's fundamental character, as holiness is the basis of His moral attributes while spirituality is the basis of His nonmoral attributes. The Holy Spirit is not a different person from the Father (Matthew 1:18-20; 10:20) but is God working in the world and in human lives (Genesis 1:2; Acts 1:5-8). In short, "Father" refers to the one God in family relationship to humans; "Son" refers to the one God incarnate; and "Spirit" refers to the one God in action. As an analogy, one human can have three significant relationships, functions, or titles—such as parent, child, and counselor—and yet be one person with a unique name. The Bible nowhere speaks of God as a "trinity" or as "three persons" but often calls Him "the Holy One."

The terms "Father" and "Son" in the New Testament serve to emphasize the true humanity of Jesus, not to make distinctions within God's being. The title of Father reminds us of God's transcendence, while the title of Son focuses on the Incarnation. Any attempt to identify two divine persons tends toward belief in two gods or else subordination of one person to the other. Defining the Son as a second divine person would result in two Sons—an eternal, divine Son who could not die and a temporal, human Son who did die. The Bible describes God as Father and Spirit before the Incarnation but as Son only in the Incarnation. While Jesus walked on earth as God incarnate, the Spirit of God continued to be transcendent and omnipresent.

The title of Word relates to God's self-expression or self-revelation. The Word is God Himself (John 1:1), particularly His thought, mind, and plan. In the person of Jesus Christ, "the Word became flesh and dwelt among us" (John 1:14). God revealed Himself in Christ.

The Deity of Jesus Christ

Jesus Christ is both God and man. He is the one God incarnate. "For in Him dwells all the fullness of the Godhead bodily" (Colossians 2:9). "God was in Christ, reconciling the world to Himself" (II Corinthians 5:19). "God was manifest in the flesh" (I Timothy 3:16). Jesus Christ is the image of the invisible God, our God and Savior, and the express image of God's own person (substance). (See II Corinthians 4:4; Colossians 1:15; Titus 2:13; Hebrews 1:3; II Peter 1:1.) When the New Testament writers called Jesus God, they confessed Jesus to be God in the Old Testament sense. Jesus accepted Thomas's confession of Him as "my Lord and my God" (John 20:28-29). He is not the incarnation of one person of a trinity but the incarnation of all the character, quality, and personality of the one God. As to His eternal deity, there can be no subordination of Jesus to anyone else, whether in essence or position.

Belief in Christ's deity is essential to salvation. Jesus said, "If you do not believe that I am He, you will die in your sins," making reference to God's name of I Am (John 8:24, 58). Only if Jesus is truly God does He have power to save from sin, for only God is the Savior and only He can forgive sin (Isaiah 43:25; 45:21-22; Mark 2:7).

All names and titles of the Deity properly apply to Jesus. He is the one God and the one Lord (John 20:28; Acts 9:5). He is the Jehovah of the Old Testament. (See Exodus 3:6, 14 with John 8:56-58; Isaiah 45:23 with Philippians 2:10-1l.) He is not only a Child and a Son but also the Mighty God and the Everlasting Father (Isaiah 9:6).

Jesus is the incarnation of the Father. Jesus said, "I and My Father are one" (John 10:30). "The Father is in Me, and I in Him" (John 10:38). "He who has seen me has seen the Father. . . . The Father who dwells in me does the works" (John 14:9-10).

Jesus is the Son of God. The term "Son" refers to Christ's human identity (as in "the Son died"), and it acknowledges the union of deity and humanity in Christ (as in "the Son will return to earth in glory"), but it is never used apart from God's incarnation. It never refers to deity alone. The terms "God the Son" and "eternal Son" are nonbiblical. The role of the Son began when Jesus was conceived miraculously in the womb of a virgin by the Holy Spirit (Luke 1:35; Galatians 4:4; Hebrews 1:5).

The Holy Spirit is the Spirit that was in Jesus Christ (Galatians 4:6; Philippians 1:19). "The Lord is the Spirit" (II Corinthians 3:17). The Holy Spirit does not come as another person but comes in another form (in spirit instead of flesh) and another relationship ("in you" instead of "with you"); the Holy Spirit is actually Jesus coming to dwell in human lives (John 14:16-18). By the Holy Spirit, Jesus fulfills His promise to dwell in our midst when we gather in His name (Matthew 18:20). Thus, all who experience a genuine work of God encounter one Spirit, not two or three. They do not experience three personalities when they worship, nor do they receive three spirits, but they are in relationship with one personal spirit being, the Spirit of Jesus.

The name of Jesus means Jehovah-Savior and thus denotes God dwelling with us (Matthew 1:21-23). It is the highest name and the only saving name (Philippians 2:9-11; Acts 4:12). It encompasses the fullness of God's revelation in the New Testament.

In eternity, we will see the one God as revealed in the person of Jesus Christ. Jesus is the One on the divine throne. (See Revelation 1:7-8, 17-18; 4:2, 8.) The vision of the One on the throne and the Lamb depicts the Incarnation and Atonement. The Lamb is not a second person but a symbol of Christ as the sacrifice for sin. The Lamb actually came out of the throne and sits on the throne (Revelation 5:6; 7:17), yet God in His sovereignty and transcendence always remains on the throne. God and the Lamb is one being with one throne, one face, and one name (Revelation 22:3-4). Only Jesus is both sovereign and sacrifice—deity and humanity—at the same time. He is the image of the invisible God, and His name is the highest name by which God is revealed. In Heaven, if we asked to see the Father apart from Jesus, the words of Jesus to Philip would still apply: "He who has seen Me has seen the Father; so how can you say, 'Show us the Father'?" (John 14:9).

The Humanity of Jesus Christ

The Scriptures proclaim Christ's genuine and complete humanity. (See Romans 1:3; Hebrews 2:14-17; 5:7-8.) He was human in body, soul, spirit, mind, and will. (See Luke 22:42; 23:46; Acts 2:31; Philippians 2:5; Hebrews 10:5, 10.) Jesus was a perfect human, with everything genuine humanity includes. Christ's true humanity does not mean He had a sinful nature. He was without sin, He committed no sin, and sin was not in Him. (See Hebrews 4:15; I Peter 2:22; I John 3:5.) He came with the kind of innocent human nature that Adam and Eve had in the beginning.

Belief in Christ's humanity is essential to salvation (I John 4:3). If God did not truly come in the flesh, then there is no blood for remission of sin, no sacrifice of atonement. The purpose of the Incarnation was to provide a holy human (not a second divine person) as the mediator between the holy God and sinful humanity (I Timothy 2:5).

Jesus acted from both divine and human viewpoints and spoke from both divine and human self-consciousness. Only as a human could Jesus be born, grow, be tempted by the devil, hunger, thirst, become weary, sleep, pray, be beaten, die, not know all things, not have all power, be inferior to God, and be a servant. Only as God could He exist from eternity, be unchanging, cast out devils by His own authority, be the bread of life, give living water, give spiritual rest, calm storms, answer prayer, heal the sick, raise His body from death, forgive sin, know all things, have all power, be identified as God, and be King of kings. In an ordinary person, these two contrasting lists would be mutually exclusive, yet the Scriptures attribute all of them to Jesus, revealing His unique identity as both God and human.

Although we must recognize both deity and humanity in Christ, it is impossible to separate the two in Him. (See John 1:1, 14; 10:30, 38; 14:10-11; 16:32.) While there was a distinction between the divine will and His human will, He always submitted the latter to the former. While on earth Jesus was fully God, not merely an anointed human. At the same time, He was fully human, not just an appearance of a human. He possessed the unlimited power, authority, and character of God. He was God by nature, by right, by identity; He was not merely deified by an anointing or indwelling. Unlike a Spirit-filled believer, the humanity of Jesus was inextricably joined with all the fullness of God's Spirit.

Christ's humanity means that everything we humans can say of ourselves, we can say of Jesus in His earthly life, except for sin. In every way that we relate to God, Jesus related to God, except that He did not need to repent or be born again. When Jesus prayed, submitted His will to the Father, and spoke about and to God, He simply acted in accordance with His authentic, genuine humanity.

Jesus is the fullness of God dwelling in perfect humanity and manifesting Himself as a perfect human being. He is not the transmutation of God into flesh, the manifestation of a portion of God, the animation of a human body by God, or God temporarily dwelling in a separate human person. Jesus Christ is the incarnation—embodiment, human personification—of the one God.

Conclusion

The beautiful message of Scripture is that our Creator became our Savior. The God against whom we sinned is the One who forgives us. God loved us so much that He came in flesh to save us. He gave of Himself; He did not send someone else. Moreover, our Creator-Savior is also the indwelling Spirit who is ever present to help us. God told us how to live and then came to live among us. He showed us how to live in the flesh and laid down His human life to purchase our salvation. Now He abides within us and enables us to live according to His will.

Jesus Christ is the one God incarnate, and in Him we have everything we need—healing, deliverance, victory, and salvation (Colossians 2:9-10). By recognizing the almighty God in Jesus Christ we restore correct biblical belief and experience apostolic power.

For Further Study

Bernard, David K. *The Oneness of God*. Rev. ed. Hazelwood, MO: Word Aflame Press, 2000.

Bernard, David K. *The Oneness View of Jesus Christ*. Hazelwood, MO: Word Aflame Press, 1994.

A Brand-New Life

God came in the flesh as Jesus Christ in order to provide salvation for His fallen creation. The Incarnation was for the purpose of the Atonement. Jesus died, was buried, and rose again in order to deliver us from all the power and effects of sin and give us a brand-new life.

The Saving Work of Jesus Christ

"All have sinned and fall short of the glory of God," and "the wages of sin is death" (Romans 3:23; 6:23). Everyone needs a Savior. The holiness of God demands that He separate from sinful humanity. Separation from the source of all life means death—physically, spiritually, and eternally—so God's holy law requires death as the penalty for sinners. Without the shedding of blood (giving of a life), there can be no release from this penalty and no fellowship with the holy God (Hebrews 9:22).

Jesus Christ is the only sinless human. As such, He alone did not deserve to die, and He alone was the perfect sacrifice. He died in our place, paid the price for us, made permanent atonement for our sins, and restored the opportunity for a relationship with God. Thus, the Bible describes Christ's death in terms of substitution, redemption, propitiation (sacrifice of atonement), and reconciliation. (See Isaiah 53:5-6; Matthew 20:28; Romans 3:24-25; 5:6-11.)

After His death, Jesus was buried, and then He arose with a glorified physical body, securing victory over death. Because of His resurrection we have overcoming power and new life in Christ as well as assurance of future immortality (Romans 8:1-11).

The Cross was the one sacrifice for all time (Hebrews 10:12). By His death, burial, and resurrection, Jesus Christ reverses all the consequences of sin. Believers enjoy many resultant blessings in this life and will receive the fullness in eternity. The benefits of Christ's work include forgiveness of sin, new spiritual life, access to God's grace, power over the devil, healing for the body, and ultimately liberation of the creation from sin's curse and eternal life for believers.

Grace and Faith

How do we receive the salvation that God has provided in Christ? "For by grace you have been saved through faith, and that not of yourselves: it is the gift of God, not of works, lest anyone should boast" (Ephesians 2:8-9). Grace means that salvation is a gift from God; it is God's work in us. We do not merit, deserve, or earn it, for it is free. We cannot save ourselves by good works or adherence to law. By His atoning death, burial, and resurrection, Jesus Christ makes the gift of salvation available. The only way to receive salvation is by faith in Christ and His saving work (Romans 1:16-17; 4:22-25).

Believing on Jesus includes believing His Word, and believing His Word includes obedience. Faith is more than mental assent or verbal profession; it includes trust, commitment, and application. Faith is alive only through response and action (James 2:14-26). Thus, we cannot separate saving faith from obedience. (See Romans 1:5; 10:16; 16:26; Hebrews 11:6-8.) Obedience to the gospel is necessary to salvation. (See Romans 6:17; II Thessalonians 1:7-10; Hebrews 5:9.) It is possible to have an initial degree of faith in Christ and still not be saved because of lack of full commitment and obedience. (See Matthew 7:21-27; John 2:23-25; 12:42-43; Acts 8:12-23.)

Faith is the means of appropriating God's grace. By faith we yield to God, obey His Word, and allow Him to perform His saving work in us. Saving faith, then, involves both acceptance of the gospel of Jesus Christ as the means of salvation and obedience to that gospel.

The Gospel and the New Birth

The gospel, which literally means "good news," is that Jesus Christ died for our sins, was buried, and rose again (I Corinthians 15:1-4). How do we obey the gospel and apply it to our lives? We find the answer in Acts 2. On the Day of Pentecost, the birthday of the New Testament church, about 120 disciples of Jesus Christ were waiting in Jerusalem as He had commanded. Suddenly, they were all filled with the Holy Spirit and miraculously began to speak with other tongues (languages) as the Spirit gave them utterance.

A large crowd gathered; some mocked while others marveled. The apostle Peter, supported by all the other apostles, responded by preaching the first gospel message. He explained that speaking in tongues was the fulfillment of a prophecy of Joel, signifying the outpouring of God's Spirit. Moreover, God's plan was for everyone to be saved by calling on the name of the Lord, whom Peter identified as Jesus. Instead of accepting Jesus, however, the people of Jerusalem crucified Him. Although he was buried, God did not allow His body to decay. Instead, the Spirit of God raised Jesus from the dead so that He has been revealed as both Lord and Messiah. In other words, Peter preached the gospel message of the death, burial, and resurrection of Jesus.

Convicted of their sins by this simple yet powerful message, the audience cried out to the apostles, "Men and brethren, what shall we do?" (Acts 2:37). Peter gave a precise, complete, and unequivocal answer: "Repent, and let every one of you be baptized in the name of Jesus Christ for the remission of sins; and you shall receive the gift of the Holy Spirit" (Acts 2:38). This answer explains how to respond to the gospel, how to believe on Jesus as Lord and Savior, how to obey and apply the gospel personally. Through repentance, we die to the old life of sin (Romans 6:1-2). Through water baptism by immersion in the name of Jesus Christ, we are buried with Christ (Romans 6:3-4). By receiving the Holy Spirit, we receive new life in Christ (Romans 7:6; 8:2).

This experience is not the work of humans, but it is God's work in us as we respond to the gospel in obedient faith. He is the one who breaks our bondage, washes away our sin, and fills us with His Spirit.

Jesus told Nicodemus, "Unless one is born again, he cannot see the kingdom of God" (John 3:3). When Nicodemus mistakenly thought He spoke of natural birth, Jesus explained that the new birth consisted of water and Spirit: "Unless one is born of water and the Spirit, he cannot enter the kingdom of God" (John 3:5). This explanation corresponds to the Pentecostal message. The birth of water is water baptism, and the birth of the Spirit is Spirit baptism. When we repent and are baptized in water, we bury the old, sinful life and the record of sin. When we receive the Holy Spirit, we begin a new, godly life by God's power. We enter into a brand-new life and become a new creation (II Corinthians 5:17).

This message also corresponds to Christ's teaching about faith. When we believe the gospel, we will repent (Mark 1:15). When we believe on Jesus, we will be baptized (Mark 16:16), and we will be filled with the Holy Spirit (John 7:37-39). This experience characterizes all who have "believed on the Lord Jesus Christ" (Acts 11:17). Through this new birth we are both justified (counted as righteous) and sanctified (set apart from sin) (I Corinthians 6:11).

Those saved in the Gospels were saved under the old covenant while they awaited the new. The new covenant did not come into effect until after Christ's ascension. (See Luke 7:28; 24:47-49; John 7:39; 16:7; Hebrews 9:14-17.) Beginning with Pentecost, the believers received the new covenant experience, including the Jews, the Samaritans, the Gentiles, the apostle Paul, and the disciples of John at Ephesus. (See Acts 2:38-41; 8:12-17; 9:17-18 with 22:16; 10:44-48; 19:1-6.) Thus Acts 2:38 is the comprehensive answer to an inquiry about New Testament conversion, expressing in a nutshell the proper response to the gospel. In short, the New Testament message of salvation is repentance from sin, water baptism in the name of Jesus Christ for the remission of sins, and receiving the Holy Spirit with the initial sign of speaking in tongues.

Repentance

Repentance is a turn from sin to God (Acts 26:18-20). It involves an intellectual change, an emotional change, and a volitional change, or decision of the will. It includes recognition of sin (Mark 2:17), confession of sin to God (I John 1:9), contrition or godly sorrow for sin (II Corinthians 7:10), and a decision to forsake sin (Proverbs 28:13). With repentance comes the willingness to make restitution for past sins if possible (Matthew 5:23-24; Luke 19:8). Repentance is the first response of faith, and it is necessary to salvation (Luke 13:3, 5; Acts 17:30).

At repentance, God enables us to break away from sinful habits and desires. Repentance allows us to have a personal relationship with God, qualifying us for baptism of water and Spirit. The work of forgiveness and remission comes through repentance and water baptism (Acts 2:38). Repentance deals with a person's present sinful lifestyle, while baptism deals with the past record and future consequences of sin.

Water Baptism

Water baptism is part of salvation (I Peter 3:21). It expresses faith in God by obedience to His Word (Acts 2:41). The scriptural mode of baptism is immersion in water, and only this method retains the biblical symbolism of baptism as a burial (Matthew 3:16; Acts 8:36-39; Romans 6:4). Faith in Christ and repentance from sin are necessary to its validity; thus infant baptism is not proper (Matthew 3:6-11; Acts 2:38; 8:37).

The biblical significance of water baptism is as follows: (1) God remits sins at water baptism, erasing the record of sin and canceling its penalty (Acts 2:38; 22:16). (2) Baptism is part of the new birth (John 3:5; Titus 3:5). (3) Baptism is part of personal identification with Christ (Romans 6:3; Galatians 3:27). (4) Baptism identifies us with Jesus' burial (Romans 6:4; Colossians 2:12). (5) Baptism is part of spiritual circumcision (Colossians 2:11-13).

The Bible teaches that baptism should be administered in the name of the Lord Jesus Christ. This means invoking the name of Jesus orally (Acts 22:16; James 2:7). It also means rebaptizing those who have been baptized another way (Acts 19:1-5). The name of Jesus in the baptismal formula expresses faith in His identity, atoning work, and saving power and authority. The name of Jesus is the only saving name, the name given for remission of sins, the highest name, and the name in which Christians are to say and do all things. (See Acts 4:12; 10:43; Philippians 2:9-11; Colossians 3:17.) Thus using Jesus' name is the proper way to fulfill all the purposes for baptism.

The Bible records five accounts of baptism in the New Testament church that describe a name or formula. In each case the name is Jesus. (See Acts 2:38; 8:16; 10:48; 19:5; 22:16.) The Epistles also allude to the Jesus Name formula. (See Romans 6:3-4; I Corinthians 1:13; 6:11; Galatians 3:27; Colossians 2:12.)

The Great Commission speaks of baptizing in "the name" of the Father, Son, and Holy Spirit (Matthew 28:19), which is a description of the Jesus Name formula. It refers to the singular name that encompasses the redemptive manifestations of the Godhead, and that name is Jesus. (See Zechariah 14:9; Matthew 1:21; John 5:43; 14:26; Revelation 22:3-4.) Moreover, Jesus is the name described in the other accounts of the Great Commission (Mark 16:17; Luke 24:47). The apostles understood and fulfilled this command by baptizing everyone in the name of Jesus Christ, and we should follow their example and teaching.

The Baptism of the Holy Spirit

Baptism with, by, in or of the Holy Ghost (Holy Spirit) is part of New Testament salvation. (See John 3:5; Romans 8:1-16; I Corinthians 12:13; Titus 3:5.) The phrase describes how the believer is immersed in and filled with God's Spirit. In Acts the terms "baptized with," "filled with," "fell upon," "poured out on," "received," and "came upon" all describe this definite, tangible, overwhelming experience. (See Acts 1:4-5; 2:4; 10:44-47; 19:6.) It is promised to all who believe on Jesus and obey His Word. (See Acts 5:32; 11:15-17; Ephesians 1:13.)

The Bible records five accounts of receiving the Holy Spirit in the New Testament church. This record establishes that the baptism of the Spirit is indeed for everyone (Luke 11:13) and is accompanied by the initial sign of tongues (Mark 16:17). Speaking in tongues means speaking supernaturally, as the Spirit gives utterance, in a language the speaker has never learned (Acts 2:1-11).

Three of the accounts explicitly describe speaking in tongues as the initial evidence of receiving the Spirit. On the Day of Pentecost, speaking in tongues was the initial sign when each individual was filled, and the apostles confirmed that it was the sign of the outpouring of the Spirit (Acts 2:4, 16-17). In Caesarea, tongues convinced skeptical, astonished Jews that the Gentiles had just received the Holy Spirit; tongues alone sufficiently identified this as the Pentecostal experience (Acts 10:44-47; 11:15-17). The Ephesian disciples, who are an example of all believers everywhere, also spoke in tongues as the first sign of receiving the Spirit (Acts 19:6).

Tongues are implicit in the other two accounts. An unnamed miraculous sign indicated the exact moment the Samaritans received the Spirit; its prior absence denoted they did not already have the Spirit despite joy, belief, and baptism, and it was so spectacular that Simon the Magician coveted the power to bestow the Spirit with this sign (Acts 8:5-19). The experience of Paul is mentioned without description (Acts 9:17), but he later testified to speaking in tongues often (I Corinthians 14:18).

The baptism of the Holy Spirit is the normal, basic New Testament experience with God. It was not just for the apostles' day but is for subsequent generations and for everyone God calls, no matter how remote in space or time (Acts 2:39). The Spirit is the rest, guide to truth, adopter, first fruits, intercessor, seal, guarantee of inheritance, and sanctifier. (See Isaiah 28:11-12; John 16:13; Romans 8:15, 23, 26; Ephesians 1:13-14; I Peter 1:2.) We receive the Spirit by repenting, opening our heart in faith, and seeking God through praise and worship. When we receive the Holy Spirit, we receive power to overcome sin, walk in holiness, and be witnesses (Acts 1:8; Romans 8:4, 13). If we let the Spirit continually fill (control and guide) us, we will bear the fruit of the Spirit and become like Christ (Galatians 5:22-23).

Conclusion

Our experience and doctrine should conform to the complete biblical pattern. Our responsibility is clear: we must act on the truth. As we respond to the gospel and believe on Jesus Christ, we will repent of our sins, be baptized in the name of Jesus Christ, and receive the gift of the Holy Spirit. We do not reject those who have not received the complete New Testament experience, but we encourage them to receive everything God has for them. There are many sincere and even repentant people, like Apollos in Acts 18 and the disciples of John at Ephesus in Acts 19, who need to be led to further truth so that they can have an apostolic new birth. Ultimately, each of us is accountable to God for our response of faith. In summary, the Bible is the sole authority for salvation; the basis of salvation is Christ's death, burial, and resurrection; salvation comes only by grace through faith in Jesus Christ; and the application of grace and the expression of faith come as a person obeys Acts 2:38, thereby receiving the new birth promised by Jesus.

For Further Study

Bernard, David K. *The New Birth*. Hazelwood, MO: Word Aflame Press, 1984.

Erickson, Gary. *The Conversion Experience: A Biblical Study of the Blood, Water and Spirit*. Hazelwood, MO: Word Aflame Press, 1987.

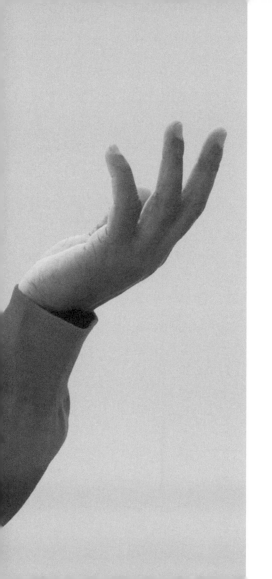

Part II

Our Practices

A Psalm of David.

Praise to God in His...

GIVE unto the LORD, O you mighty ones,
Give unto the LORD
glory and strength.
2 Give unto the LORD
the glory ²due to His name;
Worship the LORD
in ªthe ³beauty of holiness.

3 The voice of the LORD is over
the waters;
ªThe God of glory thunders;
The LORD is over many waters.
4 The voice of the LORD is
powerful;
The voice of the LORD is full of...

The Beauty of Holiness

"**W**orship the LORD in the beauty of holiness" (Psalm 29:2; 96:9). Our new life in Christ is an abundant life of love, joy, and peace as we are molded into His image. We learn to worship the Lord in all aspects and activities of life, and we learn the beauty of God's holiness.

Christian Disciplines

The Christian life is a daily walk of faith as we are led by the Holy Spirit (Romans 1:17; 8:14). Several basic disciplines are important to establish and strengthen this new life:

- *Prayer.* (See Matthew 6:5-15; Ephesians 6:18; I Thessalonians 5:17; Jude 20-21.)

- *Bible reading and study.* (See Psalm 119:11, 16, 105; II Timothy 2:15; 3:14-17.)
- *Faithful church attendance and submission to godly leadership.* (See Psalm 100; 122:1; Hebrews 10:25; 13:7, 17.)
- *Giving of tithes and offerings.* (See Malachi 3:8-12; Matthew 6:1-4; Luke 6:38; 16:10-12; II Corinthians 9:6-7.)
- *Fasting.* (See Matthew 6:16-18; 9:14-15; 17:21.)

Call to Holiness

The Bible calls followers of Christ to a life of holiness and teaches its necessity. "Pursue peace with all people, and holiness, without which no one will see the Lord" (Hebrews 12:14). The work of salvation begins with regeneration, or the new birth; continues with sanctification, a process of progressively becoming more like Christ in this life; and concludes with glorification, or resurrection with an immortal body and sinless perfection. Just as we must be born again to see the kingdom of God, so we must pursue holiness, or sanctification, in order to see the Lord. Holiness is not an option: it is a command to implement in all aspects of our lives. "As He who called you is holy, you also be holy in all your conduct, because it is written, 'Be holy, for I am holy'" (I Peter 1:15-16). We obey this command in order to please God, for we belong to Him; to communicate Christ to others; and to benefit ourselves, both now and for eternity.

Definition of Holiness

With respect to God, holiness means absolute purity, perfection, and sinlessness. With respect to God's people, holiness means conformity to the character and will of God—thinking as He thinks, loving what He loves, hating what He hates, and acting as Christ would act.

The Bible teaches a twofold definition of holiness for God's people: (1) *separation* from sin and the world's values and (2) *dedication* to God and His will. "Come out from among them and be separate, says the Lord. Do not touch what is unclean, and I will receive you. . . . Therefore, having these promises, beloved, let us cleanse ourselves from all filthiness of the flesh and spirit, perfecting holiness in the fear of God" (II Corinthians 6:17; 7:1). "I beseech you therefore, brethren, by the mercies of God, that you present your bodies a living sacrifice, holy, acceptable to God, which is your reasonable service. And do not be conformed to this world, but be transformed by the renewing of your mind, that you may prove what is that good and acceptable and perfect will of God" (Romans 12:1-2).

Holiness means to be like Christ. Instead of gratifying sinful desires, we put on Christ, letting Him be formed in us and adopting His mind (Romans 13:14; Galatians 4:19; Philippians 2:5). We judge decisions and actions by asking, What would Jesus do?

Power to Live a Holy Life

Holiness comes by faith, love, and walking after the Spirit. First, as with all aspects of salvation, we receive sanctification by grace through faith (Ephesians 2:8-9). Holiness is not a means of earning salvation but a result of salvation. We cannot manufacture our own holiness; we are partakers of God's holiness (Hebrews 12:10). Genuine faith results in obedience (Romans 1:5; 16:26; James 2:14-26). Thus, if we truly believe God, we will believe and obey His Word, which in turn will lead to the pursuit of holiness. If we deliberately and persistently disobey God's Word, then we are no longer walking in faith.

Second, if we truly love God, we will obey God's commandments (John 14:15, 23). Without love, all attempts to live for God are vain (I Corinthians 13:1-13). When we truly love God, we will actively hate evil (Psalm 97:10), and we will seek to become like our holy God. Love is stricter and more demanding than law, for love always goes further than duty. Love for God will cause us to draw closer to God than law will, both in attitudes and in disciplined living. Love will cause us to avoid everything that displeases God or hinders a closer walk with Him. Love rejects anything that is incompatible with godliness or not conducive to spiritual life, even though no law specifically labels it as sin. In this way, the principle of love leads to greater holiness than does the law of Moses or any other codification of rules. Love dominates all actions and all relationships. All the law is summed up in love: we are to love God with all our being and to love our fellow humans as we love ourselves (Matthew 22:36-40; Romans 13:9-10).

Third, through the Spirit's guidance and power, we can overcome sin and live righteously (Romans 8:2-4; Galatians 5:16). We have freedom from sin's dominion—the power to choose not to sin (John 8:34-36; Romans 6:1-25). We will not continue to live in sin; indeed, when we act according to our new identity we cannot sin (I John 3:9). We still have the ability to sin and we still struggle with the inward nature of sin (Galatians 5:16-17; I John 1:8; 2:1), but as long as we let the Holy Spirit lead us we will not sin.

Holiness is not an external law but an integral part of our new identity. The Spirit places God's moral law within us, not written on stone tablets but in our hearts (Hebrews 10:16). We do not merely follow an external list of rules, but we follow the Holy Spirit within us. We pursue holiness because that is who we are and want to be. We abstain from sin and worldliness because it is anathema to our new nature. We still struggle against the desires of the old nature, but it is an internal struggle. Nobody imposes rules on us; we restrict our flesh because we wish to follow the Spirit. We understand the beauty of holiness.

Following holiness requires personal effort; it is not automatic. We must yield to the working of God's Spirit. We must implement spiritual disciplines, establish guidelines for conduct, submit to God, and resist temptation. "Make every effort to be found spotless, blameless, and at peace with him" (II Peter 3:14, NIV). "Work out your own salvation with fear and trembling. For it is God who works in you both to will and to do for His good pleasure" (Philippians 2:12-13). God gives believers both the desire and the power to live righteously. He performs the work in us, but we must reverently and watchfully allow that work to be manifested. As an analogy, farmers are totally dependent upon God for sunshine, rain, and the miracle of life in the seed. Nevertheless, they will not have a crop unless they till, plant, tend, and harvest. In short, we cannot do what God must do, but God will not do what we can do.

Principles of Holiness

Holiness is both inward and outward (I Corinthians 6:19-20; II Corinthians 7:1). It includes attitudes, thoughts, and spiritual stewardship but also actions, appearance, and physical stewardship. Both aspects are essential.

We must not love this ungodly world system, identify with it, become attached to the things in it, or participate in its sinful pleasures and activities (James 1:27; 4:4; I John 2:15). We must avoid three major areas of sin: the lust of the flesh, the lust of the eyes, and the pride of life (I John 2:16). We must discipline ourselves, and we must abstain from every form of evil (I Corinthians 9:24-27; I Thessalonians 5:22). The Christian's daily goal is to overcome sin (John 5:14; 8:11). We are not to sin, but if we do, we can receive forgiveness by repentance and confession to God (I John 1:9; 2:1).

The life of holiness is one of continual growth toward perfection (Matthew 5:48; II Corinthians 7:1; Philippians 3:12-16). No one is perfect in an absolute sense, but we can be perfect in a relative sense by developing properly at every stage and becoming mature. God expects increasing production of spiritual fruit (John 15:1-8). Our goal is not to conform to the expectations of others but to follow the leading of God through His Word, Spirit, and church.

All of us, and particularly new believers, need space and time to "grow in the grace and knowledge of our Lord and Savior Jesus Christ" (II Peter 3:18).

God has given three teachers of holiness. First, all holiness teachings come from the Bible, the inspired Word of God. Second, the Holy Spirit teaches us by internal promptings and convictions. Third, anointed preachers and teachers proclaim and apply the Word. God has given pastors for the oversight, care, and equipping of the church.

Some teachings are explicitly stated in Scripture. Others are practical applications of scriptural principles for our culture, time, and place. There may be some differences of opinion on exactly how to apply a principle or where to draw a line. Nevertheless, it is important for pastors to make practical applications, or else the principles will be neglected. Likewise, for our spiritual protection, for the unity of the body, and for a clear witness to the community, it is important for us to follow the teaching and admonition of godly pastors.

The Christian life is one of liberty rather than legalism, which means basing salvation on works or imposing nonbiblical rules. We have freedom from sin, freedom from the law, and freedom to act as we will in nonmoral matters. Christian liberty does not negate the responsibility to follow moral law and scriptural teaching, however (Romans 6:15; Galatians 5:13). Moreover, the Bible presents guidelines for the proper exercise of liberty even in nonmoral matters: (1) Do everything to the glory of God (I Corinthians 10:31). (2) Avoid anything detrimental, not beneficial, or a "weight" that holds us back (I Corinthians 6:12; 10:23; Hebrews 12:1). (3) Avoid anything that will gain dominance over us (I Corinthians 6:12). (4) Avoid anything that will harm others (Romans 14:13-21; I Corinthians 8:9-13).

Practical Applications

Holiness begins in the heart with attitudes and thoughts and extends to our way of life, behavior, appearance, and speech. We will briefly discuss some important areas in which biblical, and therefore universal and unchanging, principles of holiness apply.

Attitudes. (See Galatians 5:19-23; Ephesians 4:23-32.) The essence of holiness is to bear the fruit of the Spirit, which includes love, joy, peace, longsuffering, kindness, goodness, faithful, gentleness, and self-control. As Christians, we learn to forgive, obey authority, be thankful, not let anything offend us, and not be busybodies in others' lives. We put away evil attitudes such as hatred, malice, wrath, envy, jealousy, covetousness, bitterness, pride, prejudice, vengeance, strife, and discord. Holiness also includes justice and mercy in personal and social relationships.

Thoughts. (See Matthew 15:18-20; II Corinthians 10:5; Philippians 4:8.) We are what we think, and we become what we allow our minds to dwell upon. We are to think on true, noble, just, pure, lovely, commendable, virtuous, and praiseworthy things. We cast out temptations and evil thoughts, taking every thought captive to obey Christ.

The tongue. (See Colossians 4:6; James 1:26; 3:1-2; 4:11; 5:12.) We employ wholesome, gracious speech. Thus, we avoid tale bearing, backbiting, slander, sowing discord, swearing by oath, using the Lord's name in vain, pronouncing curses, reviling, lying, idle words, and suggestive, indecent, or obscene speech.

The eye. (See Psalm 101:2-3; 119:37; Matthew 6:22-23.) The eye is the gate of the soul and the primary source of input for the mind. We guard ourselves against reading or viewing things that are sensual, vulgar, immoral, or saturated with violence. Because of the widespread display of evil in modern media, we must be particularly mindful of the dangers associated with television ownership, movies, and the Internet.

Appearance (adornment, dress, and hair). (See Deuteronomy 22:5; I Corinthians 11:1-16; I Timothy 2:8-10; I Peter 3:1-5.) The appearance reflects the inner self, both to God and to others. Worldly styles promote lust of the flesh, lust of the eyes, and pride of life, molding both wearer and society in ungodly ways. Biblical principles here include modesty, avoidance of personal ornamentation, moderation in cost, and distinction between male and female in dress and hair.

Stewardship of the body. (See I Corinthians 3:16-17; 6:12, 19-20.) The body is the temple of the Spirit, so we promotion moderation and stewardship in diet, exercise, and rest. We do not use things that harm or defile the body, cause intoxication, or cause addiction.

Sanctity of marriage. (See I Corinthians 6:9-11; Colossians 3:5; Hebrews 13:4.) Marriage is the lifelong commitment of a man and a woman. Divorce is not God's plan but is a result of human sin. Sexual relationships are wholesome in marriage but sinful outside of marriage. We are to guard against lustful thoughts and actions.

Sanctity of human life. (See Exodus 20:13; Matthew 5:39, 44.) Humans were created in God's image; thus, we seek to avoid violence and bloodshed. Abortion and assisted suicide are wrongful takings of human life.

Honesty. (See Mark 10:19.) The Bible promotes integrity and rejects all dishonesty, including lying, theft, fraud, refusal to pay debts, extortion, bribery, and cheating.

Godly fellowship. (See Matthew 18:15-18; I Corinthians 5:9-6:8; 15:33.) We need wholesome fellowship, unity in the church, mutual accountability, and mutual submission. We should not associate closely with so-called believers who habitually indulge in sinful activities. We resolve internal disagreements within the church, not by secular lawsuits.

Worldly activities. (See I Thessalonians 5:22; Titus 3:3; I John 2:15.) We conduct activities in a wholesome atmosphere and seek to be a godly example in everything. With this in mind, we maturely regulate amusements, music, sports, and games.

Conclusion

Holiness is an integral part of the salvation of the whole person from sin's power and effects. It is a joyful privilege; a part of abundant life; a blessing from God's grace; a glorious life of freedom and power. The life of holiness fulfills God's original intention and design for humanity. For the Spirit-filled believer who loves God, holiness is the normal—indeed the only—way to live.

For Further Study

Bernard, David K, and Loretta Bernard. *In Search of Holiness*. Rev. ed. Hazelwood, MO: Word Aflame Press, 2005.

Bernard, David K. *Practical Holiness: A Second Look*. Hazelwood, MO: Word Aflame Press, 1986.

Wagner, Lori. *The Girl in the Dress: Uncovering the Mystery of Modesty*. Hazelwood, MO: Ladies Ministries UPCI, 2010.

CHAPTER 6

Then Sings My Soul:
The Practice of Worship

After Jesus had sent his disciples into the marketplace of Sychar to purchase food, He made His way to the ancient well dug by the patriarch Jacob. The klatch of women who came daily to the well had already made their way home. A solitary Samaritan woman, relieved that the earlier crowd had dissipated, hurried to the well. She didn't want to deal with the disdainful glances and hushed conversation of women who disapproved of her choices. She was surprised and shocked when Jesus asked her for a drink of water—surprised by His presence at the well and shocked that a Jewish man would speak with her. Many years earlier a deep rift had developed between the Jews and Samaritans, and Jews took great care to avoid Samaritans. Jesus took the opportunity created by her astonishment to turn the conversation in a spiritual direction. Before long they were talking about worship. Over time and through misunderstandings the Jews and Samaritans had developed different worship practices. Jesus pointed to a better day coming in the near future, when worship would reach a new dimension. While outlining these changes He reminded the Samaritan woman that the Father seeks true worshipers. (See John 4:19-24.) He still is today.

In many ways, the Samaritan woman was a prototypical human. She was not only flawed, she was a worshiper. Since the dawn of civilizations humans have been worshipers. Regardless of the geographic location, ethnic make-up, and the progression of cultures, people have found a way to worship a perceived higher power. Even with the advances of science that partially unveil the mysteries of life and the progress of technology that effectively shrinks the world, this still holds true today. In spite of predictions that religious faith would disappear, it has remained resilient. Perhaps this is because we were created to be worshipers.

The act of worship is the rule and not the exception in human existence. So the question is not *will* humans worship, but rather *who* and *how* will they worship. The object of worship is infinitely more important than the act of worship. The first two injunctions of the Ten Commandments address this issue. "You shall have no other gods before Me. You shall not make for yourself a carved image—any likeness of anything that is in heaven above, or that is in the earth beneath, or that is in the water under the earth; you shall not bow down to them nor serve them. For I, the LORD your God, am a jealous God" (Exodus 20:3-5). Idolatry can be defined as the act of worshiping anything other than

God or, as the third commandment forbids, an image of God Himself. Only God is to be the object of worship. Anything less than this makes worship without value.

After deciding whom to worship, the next decision is how to worship. This is a more difficult question than the first. There is only one being worthy of worship—that is God. However, the Bible does not outline a singular way in which to worship Him. It does, however, provide broad parameters for worship. For example, not long after life began outside of Eden, both Cain and Abel, in an act of worship, brought a sacrifice to offer to God. Abel's sacrifice was accepted; Cain's was rejected. The biblical narrative does not provide insight into the reasons for the different outcomes and to speculate would not be productive. This much we know; there was a right way and a wrong way to approach God. Paul's instruction to the Corinthian church in I Corinthians 14 also demonstrates the idea of right and wrong worship practices.

Worship at an altar of sacrifice was a central feature of Old Testament worship. The patriarchs of Genesis provided this priestly function for their extended families. As the nation of Israel began to develop, the high priest became the person primarily responsible for this task. First the Tabernacle and then the Temple were constructed as places to offer sacrifices. They were not only located physically in a central location, they were spiritually the center of Jewish life.

New Testament Worship

This aspect of worship changed in the New Testament. Instead of periodic offerings of a lamb or some other sacrificial animal, Jesus Christ became the sacrificial lamb who took away the sin of the world once and for all. This is the gospel or the good news. The blood of bulls and goats, which could not completely atone for sin, were no longer necessary.

What then did New Testament worship look like? The Book of Acts, which is the primary narrative of the earliest church, offers hints and suggestions but does not attempt to describe the workings of a worship event. The earliest Christians continued to frequent the Temple in Jerusalem so it is safe to assume some similarity between the worship of their Jewish past and their new faith, which emerged from that background. In addition to their Jewish worship experiences, what we know as the Old Testament was their only Scripture. It would seem logical that they would look to it for direction. If you strip the animal sacrifices and the associated rituals from Old Testament worship what would be left?

Music

Music played a key role in worship. The Book of Psalms is a collection of songs. As evidenced by the wide variety of lyrics found in Psalms, music expresses the emotions of the heart in a richer way than purely rational reflection. The singing of psalms was accompanied by musical instruments. In fact, musicians were urged to play skillfully. (See Psalm 33:3.) Twice Paul references music—and different kinds of music—as part of New Testament worship. (See Ephesians 5:19 and Colossian 3:16.) Music continues to play a significant role in worship today. Almost any style of music can be utilized for worship—it is primarily the content of the lyrics that makes music Christian.

In addition to underscoring the role of music in worship, the Book of Psalms highlights an exuberance often associated with worship. Worship is to be heartfelt. A wide array of emotional responses is on display in Psalms. As you read through the Psalms you encounter weeping, laughter, and joyful celebration. The most common worship exhortation in Psalms is to joyfully celebrate God and His goodness. Celebration takes on many forms and is often culturally mediated. Worship in a village in South Africa will probably look somewhat different than it will in a suburban community in North America. However, the object of worship will remain the same.

Preaching

New Testament worship also included the proclamation of the Word of God. So critical is this aspect of worship that early in the history of the church the apostles chose deacons to help them with the administrative functions of the church so they could set aside time to prepare for the ministry of the Word. (See Acts 6:1-4.) Preaching or proclamation of the Word of God is fundamental to worship. It helps the church better understand the God they worship and urges hearers to respond to both the gospel's offers and demands. Preaching reminds and reveals to hearers biblical truths.

Good preaching illustrates the communal nature of worship. The preacher delivers God's Word and the congregation responds to that Word. Both actions mutually strengthen each other and give public witness to the covenant between God and His church.

Prayer

"Now Peter and John went up together to the temple at the hour of prayer, the ninth hour" (Acts 3:1). God has always been interested in conversation with His people. In the Garden of Eden, He came down in the cool of the evening to visit with Adam and Eve. Woven throughout the Old Testament are accounts of people praying in community and by themselves. In the Gospels Jesus prayed and taught His disciples to do the same. On at least one occasion He spoke about the value of private prayer—the prayer closet. Prayer does indeed hold great value for a Christian's devotional life.

Public prayer draws a community together. It reminds the gathered group that the ultimate source of the answers to our questions and needs is God alone. Paul's prayers often included in the beginning section of his epistles demonstrate the value of pastoral prayers.

Although Jesus did give His disciples a sample pattern for prayer, the very nature of prayer resists a highly ritualized practice. Heartfelt prayer is often spontaneous. To be authentic it must flow from the life of the one praying.

Public prayer should balance an individual's freedom to pray with a larger concern for structure and order.

Giving

When David began the process of creating a permanent home for the Ark of the Covenant, he found a piece of ground he felt was a suitable location. Ornan, the owner of the land, offered to give it to David. David refused Ornan's offer, insisting that he could not worship in a place that cost him nothing. (See II Samuel 24:23-25 and I Chronicles 24:23-25.)

Giving is part of worship. It helps to remind the giver that God is the source of all blessings. Tithing a portion of one's income grows out of this recognition. Because God is a giving God, we reflect His nature when we give. The Bible is filled with encouragements to give. One of Paul's primary tasks as he traveled across Asia Minor and southern Europe was to raise an offering for the Jerusalem church. He did so unapologetically.

In addition to the giving of finances, the Bible encourages us to give of our time. The Sabbath or day of rest and renewal was initiated by God to help humans restore balance into their lives.

Communion

The nearest aspect of New Testament worship to the Old Testament sacrificial altar is the celebration of communion. On the eve of His crucifixion,

Jesus celebrated the Passover supper with His disciples. As they dined, He prepared them for the coming events, including His death. He shared with the disciples broken bread and fruit of the vine, likening these two items to His soon-to-be-broken body and shed blood. He asked they continue the practice in memory of His sacrifice. This act of worship is called the Lord's Supper or communion and it continues to be practiced today. It is both a time of remembrance for His sacrifice and a celebration of that sacrifice.

Like almost all aspects of worship, the Lord's Supper is to be celebrated in a community of believers. It is possible to see in communion both the vertical and horizontal orientations of worship. Believers look upward as they reflect on the idea that Jesus gave His life so that they might have abundant life. They look to each other as they share the elements of communion and are reminded that everyone is equal at the foot of the Cross. If this horizontal nature is lost, then the act itself loses much of its power. Paul's rebuke of the Corinthian church for their mishandling of communion reveals the importance of both orientations to this act of worship. (See I Corinthians 11:17-34.)

The vertical and horizontal aspects of communion are replicated in most acts of worship. Take for example the psalmist's simple call to worship: "Enter into His gates with thanksgiving, and into His courts with praise. Be thankful to Him, and bless His name" (Psalm 100:4). Thanksgiving is to be directed to God. After all, He is the giver of all good gifts. "Every good gift and every perfect gift is from above, and comes down from the Father of lights" (James 1:17). Authentic thanksgiving can only be given from a thankful heart. This is true in our relationship to God and in our human relationships. A mother can insist that her child always says "thank-you" when he receives a gift. But she cannot compel him to be thankful, because thankfulness only grows in the heart. A heart that produces thanksgiving for God's good gift will by its very nature exhibit thanksgiving in his human relationships. If a person can freely express genuine thankfulness in human relationships, his relationship to God will also be seasoned with thankfulness. If he is not thankful toward God, then he will probably not see reasons to be thankful for human gifts as well.

God-honoring worship is infectious. It invites others to participate as well. This is only magnified when the Spirit of the Lord begins to move among worshipers. Lives begin to be changed. Burdens are lifted and purpose is renewed. Good worship is touched by a little of the mystery of the supernatural. It is a holy encounter. When Moses observed the burning bush he removed his shoes because he felt he was standing on holy ground. Worship still calls us to a holy place and invites us to create a sacred space in our lives.

All of Life Is Worship

This chapter has examined the broad parameters of worship. We have looked at particular activities that bring honor to God and nurture to ourselves and other believers. In the previous paragraph we have made an appeal for the creation of a sacred space. On one level this is too narrow of a definition of worship because all of life is worship. In reality, all of our actions and attitudes have the possibility of bringing honor to God. It is counterproductive to segment our lives into sacred and secular categories. We are called to live more holistically. We cannot be a saint on Sunday and live like there is no God on Monday. Paul encouraged us to "present your bodies a living sacrifice, holy, acceptable to God, which is your reasonable service" (Romans 12:1).

One of the reasons Jesus proved to be such a challenge to the religious leaders of His day was because He refused to live His life inside a predetermined religious box. He was tired of the disconnect He saw in people for whom religion was only a ritual. He knew that life was richer and deeper than this. He wanted to draw all people, regardless of their backgrounds, to God. He still calls us to authentic worship today.

Around the globe today people are worshiping God. Some will even use words. From deep within the human heart the desire to worship will compel people to reach upward and outward to God and His people.

In the words of a well-loved hymn of the church, "Then sings my soul… how great thou art!"

For Further Study

Erickson, Gary. *Pentecostal Worship: A Biblical and Practical Approach.* Hazelwood, MO: Word Aflame Press, 1989.

CHAPTER 7

Gifts of the Spirit

Every believer is a vital part of the church and should participate in the life of the congregation. The Bible speaks of the church as the body of Christ. (See Romans 12; I Corinthians 12.) It is one body but has many members with different functions. Thus, we strive for unity and celebrate diversity at the same time. God has endowed the members with special abilities and ministries for the benefit of the body as a whole. Each of us should identify our particular gifts and exercise them to the best of our ability.

We will look at three lists of gifts to the New Testament church. These lists are not exhaustive but representative or illustrative of the ways God uses individuals in His church. After a brief overview of each list, we will focus on the supernatural spiritual gifts because of their special, miraculous nature.

Service Gifts

Romans 12 describes abilities, talents, or functions that God gives to believers to serve the body. While some natural human abilities correspond to this list, at least in part, God is the one who bestows these abilities, and only by His grace can they operate in the spiritual realm. To some extent, every mature Christian should be able to function in these areas, yet each has some area of special strength as given by God.

> **1.** *Prophecy:* speaking under divine anointing to edify others. This gift includes testimony, proclamation, and preaching.
> **2.** *Ministry:* service to others, particularly assisting in various areas of the church.
> **3.** *Teaching:* instruction and training.
> **4.** *Exhortation:* giving encouragement or comfort.
> **5.** *Giving:* sharing material blessings.
> **6.** *Leading:* providing direction, guidance, and influence.
> **7.** *Showing mercy:* being merciful and kind.

Leadership Offices

Ephesians 4 identifies special leaders that God has given to the church. While Romans 12 speaks of abilities or functions, Ephesians 4 speaks of offices, using titles to designate recognized leaders. God gives these leaders to the church for the equipping of all believers, so that everyone can find a place of service. They inspire, motivate, disciple, instruct, and train the members of the body so that everyone can be productive. The result is the edification, or building up, of the whole body. The church functions effectively, becomes established in truth, and grows into maturity.

1. *Apostle:* one sent with a commission, messenger, ambassador, commissioner. Although no one can take the place of the twelve apostles of the Lamb (Revelation 21:14), who were eyewitnesses of Christ, others fulfill an apostolic office by serving as pioneer missionaries and leaders of other ministers.

2. *Prophet:* one who imparts special messages or direction from God. Prophets frequently communicate messages concerning God's plan for the future or the church's need to take action in God's plan.

3. *Evangelist:* literally, one who preaches the gospel; specifically, one whose primary ministry is to proclaim the good news to the unsaved.

4. *Pastor:* literally, "shepherd"; one who leads and cares for God's people. The Bible also speaks of pastors as bishops (literally, "overseers") and elders.

5. *Teacher:* one who instructs in God's Word.

Supernatural Spiritual Gifts

In I Corinthians 12 we find nine supernatural or miraculous gifts that result from the direct operation of the Holy Spirit. We use the word *supernatural* from a human perspective to indicate the immediate intervention of God. From a spiritual perspective, of course, divine intervention is normal, for God created the universe and sustains it by His grace. These gifts are signs that attest to God's work in the church and empowerments that further the mission of the church.

1. *Word of wisdom:* a special portion of divine insight, judgment, or guidance for a particular need.
2. *Word of knowledge:* a special portion of divine information for a particular need.
3. *Faith:* a special ability to trust God, or to inspire trust in God, for a particular need or circumstance.
4. *Gifts of healings:* various forms of miraculous cure or restoration from illnesses, diseases, injuries, and other impairments.
5. *Working of miracles:* the direct intervention of God transcending the typical operations of nature in a situation, working through or with a human vessel.
6. *Prophecy:* a miraculous utterance directly from God in the language of the speaker and hearers.
7. *Discerning of spirits:* a special ability to perceive the spiritual motivations for an action, or what type of spirit is at work.
8. *Different kinds of tongues:* a miraculous utterance in one or more languages unknown to the speaker.
9. *Interpretation of tongues:* a miraculous ability to translate or explain the meaning of a public utterance in tongues.

The apostolic church was characterized by signs and wonders that attracted people to the gospel and enabled the church to growth (Acts 2:43; 4:33).

Hebrews 2:3-4 underscores the supernatural character of these gifts: "How shall we escape if we neglect so great a salvation, which at the first began to be spoken by the Lord, and was confirmed to us by those who heard Him, God also bearing witness both with signs and wonders, with various miracles, and gifts of the Holy Spirit, according to His own will?"

The Operation of Spiritual Gifts

The originator is the Holy Spirit. (See I Corinthians 12:4-11.) While the gifts differ, the one true God is the author of them all. He is the one who performs the work by His Spirit.

The gifts are supernatural. This passage of Scripture describes them as "works" of God and as the "manifestation of the Spirit." It is a mistake to define them in terms of natural human abilities.

They are given according to God's will. There is great value in learning about spiritual gifts and learning to yield to God's Spirit so that we are prepared for God to use us. But no human can grant such a gift to someone or exercise such a gift at will. God is the one who bestows and enables the gifts according to His sovereign purpose. (See I Corinthians 12:11; Hebrews 2:4.)

It is God's will for these gifts to operate in every local body of believers until the second coming of Christ (I Corinthians 1:2, 7). We are to seek them and not despise or forbid them (I Corinthians 12:31; 14:39). A healthy, fully functional church will desire and acquire all of God's gifts for His body.

Every Spirit-filled believer can potentially operate any spiritual gift as the need arises. Not everyone will regularly exercise one of the nine gifts, and probably no one will regularly exercise them all, but all should yield to the working of God's Spirit so as to be available for any manifestation that God chooses. We open our hearts to His work through sensitivity, faith, and humility.

The ultimate purpose of the spiritual gifts is to exalt the Lord. We should always draw attention to what God, not a human, is doing. It is troubling when the primary emphasis is on a human personality or the exercise of a particular gift in itself. For instance, gifts of healing are often effective in building faith and sparking a revival that leads many people to salvation. (See Acts 3:1-11; 4:4.) But if a meeting or a ministry focuses on healing while neglecting the message of salvation, then God's purpose in granting healing is not fully accomplished.

The gifts are bestowed for times of special need. In the church, they should be normal, not abnormal; expected, not unexpected. They do not operate continually, however. To illustrate, in the Gospels and Acts multitudes were healed and a number of people were raised from the dead. Nevertheless, all the members of the early church eventually died without being raised again, and presumably most died of some illness or disease that was not healed.

There is a diversity of gifts, but their immediate purpose is to build up the entire body (I Corinthians 12:4-6, 12-26). Different people exercise different gifts, but all should do so for the good of the body. We value the unique contributions that each person makes, while recognizing that God does not bestow gifts primarily to benefit individuals but to benefit the whole.

The purpose of the spiritual gifts is not to establish doctrine, replace spiritual leadership in the church, or replace the daily guidance from God that we receive through prayer and submission of heart, mind, and will. Those who try to use spiritual gifts as a substitute for these things are in error. Each Christian must study God's Word, follow godly leaders, walk by faith, grow in spiritual wisdom and knowledge, and develop an understanding of God's will.

We must exercise gifts according to God's Word so that we do not we misuse the gifts. The gifts are subject to the control of the user (I Corinthians 14:32). We have a responsibility to use them as God has intended and instructed. Everything should be done decently and in divine order, which involves submission to spiritual authority (I Corinthians 14:40).

Specifically, we must operate all gifts with love for God and each other, not out of pride, strife, manipulation, or attempt to control others. Love is the only acceptable motivation; without love, they are worthless. (See I Corinthians 13:1-8.)

The manifestation of spiritual gifts is not necessarily a sign of spiritual maturity in the recipient. Someone may have faith to receive a gift but not be doctrinally sound or spiritually mature in other ways. We should not focus on the individual who exercises or receives a gift, but an awesome display of spiritual gifts should remind us of the grace and power of the Giver.

Gifts of Healing

Healing is more prominent in Scripture than many other gifts, probably because it is more visible, ministers more directly to urgent human needs, is particularly effective in evangelism, and demonstrates God's plan of salvation for the whole person. Jesus Christ purchased our physical healing as part of the Atonement (Isaiah 53:4-5; Matthew 8:16-17). "Jesus Christ is the same yesterday, today, and forever" (Hebrews 13:8). What He did for the early church He will do for the church today.

Healing is not automatic, however. Some benefits of the Atonement are immediate, while others are future. Some New Testament Christians suffered from sickness for a time without receiving immediate healing. (See Philippians 2:25-27; I Timothy 5:23; II Timothy 4:20.) Christians are not immune from the diseases, trials, and tribulations of everyday life. Moreover, sometimes healing comes instantly, while sometimes it is gradual or progressive. (See Mark 8:22-25; Luke 17:12-14.)

God does not always answer prayer in the way we desire or expect; nevertheless we trust in Him. (See Job 13:15; James 1:2-4.) God does not prevent all trials, but He always provides grace to sustain and deliver us in time of trial. (See I Corinthians 10:13; II Corinthians 12:7-9.) Faith is not only manifested in miraculous deliverance; faith can be equally seen in patient endurance through trials (Daniel 3:17-18; Hebrews 11:35-39). We should pray and believe for healing, but if we are sick for a time we can use whatever means He has made available for alleviation of suffering and progress toward recovery. It is not wrong to seek help from doctors or medicine, for they assist the body in regaining the healing function that God created us to have.

Why do some people not receive healing? There can be several reasons, including their lack of faith, their own action or inaction that caused sickness, and the general versus specific will of God. Sometimes God may use an illness to accomplish a specific purpose in their lives or the lives of others, and at some point there is "a time to die" (Ecclesiastes 3:2).

When someone is sick, we should pray for him or her to recover (James 5:14-16). We have assurance that God will hear and answer this prayer—but in His manner and time, not necessarily ours. He may heal instantly, begin a gradual process of healing, use what we consider natural means, heal later, give grace through a time of sickness, or allow the person to die in faith and receive the answer in the resurrection. These considerations should not stop us from believing God for healing, however. We should pray in faith and live in faith. When we do, we will observe and experience God's miraculous healing power on a regular basis. Most of all, we will realize that God does not always act as we wish or expect but works all things together for our good (Romans 8:28).

Gifts of Utterance

Because of their public nature, the gifts of utterance (prophecy, tongues, and interpretation of tongues) are also more noticeable than most gifts, and they are potentially subject to misunderstanding or misuse. For this reason, I Corinthians 14 provides instructions on their proper use.

While God is infallible, humans are not. Sometimes they mistake their own ideas for God's prompting, and sometimes they mistakenly share something publicly that God gave for them alone. Moreover, when God uses people for a prophetic utterance, they do not thereby have the authority to interpret and apply it on behalf of others. When prophets speak, the listeners must exercise discernment and evaluate the significance of the prophecy for themselves. (See Acts 21:4, 10-14; I Corinthians 14:29.)

As discussed in Chapter 4, speaking in tongues is the initial sign of receiving the Holy Spirit. Subsequently, it is a great blessing and benefit in personal devotions (I Corinthians 14:4, 14-18). In congregational meetings, when there is a public message in tongues we should seek an interpretation. If none is forthcoming, the speaker should not continue to address the audience in tongues, but he or she can continue to pray quietly in tongues for personal benefit (I Corinthians 14:27-28). When it is time for the whole congregation to pray or worship, then all have the opportunity to speak directly to God either in their own language or in tongues.

Conclusion

We should earnestly desire all the gifts of the Spirit, particularly those that will benefit the whole church under the particular circumstances. We should not forbid or discourage any spiritual gift, as long as it is used to bless everyone. We should conduct all spiritual activities in a decent and orderly manner so as to fulfill the supreme objectives of glorifying Jesus Christ and edifying His body.

God "is able to do exceedingly abundantly above all that we ask or think, according to the power that works in us" (Ephesians 3:20). As Spirit-filled believers, we should exercise simple faith to receive God's miraculous gifts and to stir up the gifts He has already placed in our midst. Whenever special needs arise, we should believe that He can work through us. In this way the gifts of the Spirit become vital tools for strengthening the church and reaching the world with the gospel of Jesus Christ.

For Further Study

Bernard, David K. *Spiritual Gifts*. Hazelwood, MO: Word Aflame Press, 1997.

CHAPTER 8

To the End of the Earth— The Pentecostal Mission

I magine the panic that gripped the hearts of Mary and Joseph when they discovered that their twelve-year-old son was missing. Their family had been in Jerusalem for a religious festival and now they were returning to their Galilean village. But they could not find their son, Jesus, so they returned to Jerusalem fiercely hoping that nothing had harmed Him. When they finally found Him, He was in deep conversation with the rabbis. As you might expect from panicked parents, they scolded Him for the anxiety He had caused them. His response, "I must be about My Father's business," foreshadowed His sense of calling. (See Luke 2:41-49.) Even from a young age, Jesus understood He had a mission.

Almost two decades later, this same sense of mission caused Him to lay down His carpenter's tools and launch a public ministry. Sprinkled liberally throughout His conversations were reminders of His sense of mission. He said things such as "the Son of Man has come to seek and to save that which was lost" (Luke 19:10). He developed parables about lost sheep, lost coins, and lost sons. (See Luke 15:1-32.) And when He invited a few Galilean fishermen to join Him, He promised them that they would become fishers of men. He invited them to be partners in ministry. (See Matthew 4:19 and Mark 1:17.)

There was one key piece of His mission that only He could do. Only He could become the sacrificial lamb that made it possible for humans to live without the penalty of sin. He willingly gave His sinless life so that we could enter a full relationship with God. It is easy to see how key this was in the Gospel accounts as you observe how each of the accounts hurried to the Passion Week, the week of His crucifixion and resurrection. The Gospel writers understood that this was the ultimate hinge of history. His death, burial, and resurrection changed the world. Salvation was now available for all of humankind. Matthew closed his Gospel with what has become known as the Great Commission. In it Jesus challenged His disciples to go and make disciples of all nations (Matthew 28:19).

Apostolic Mission

The opening chapter of the Book of Acts echoed this challenge. The gospel was to be preached to the end of the earth. However, two things needed to be changed before this would be possible. The first happened in the opening chapters of Acts. In Acts 1, Jesus addressed His disciples just before His ascension, and promised them that shortly the Spirit would be poured out on all flesh. The Spirit would empower them to carry the gospel around the world. "But you shall receive power when the Holy Spirit has come upon you; and you shall be witnesses to Me in Jerusalem, and in all Judea and Samaria, and to the end of the earth" (Acts 1:8). Chapter 2 describes that Pentecostal outpouring. On the Day of Pentecost the Spirit fell not only on the disciples, but also on many Jewish pilgrims who had traveled to Jerusalem to celebrate the Feast.

The second change took more time. The disciples had difficulty in seeing beyond the Jewish world. They filtered the words of Jesus through a lens that had a very narrow focal length. However, by the tenth chapter of Acts they had pushed, or more accurately, they had been pushed through their cultural barriers. The gospel was being preached to the Samaritans and then to the Gentile world.

Luke organized his narrative of the new church around Acts 1:8. His account of the rapid expansion of the church first documented the events in Jerusalem, then Samaria, and finally it followed Paul as he traveled into Europe. The church, sometimes pushed along by persecution, was always on the move. Paul, in particular, saw himself as an apostle to the Gentiles and he aggressively spread the message. The early church was a missionary church. It follows then that any church attempting to follow the apostolic pattern would be a missionary church.

The Modern Pentecostal Movement

Since the modern Pentecostal movement grew out of a desire to restore the church to its apostolic roots, it was also a missionary church. However, the desire to follow the apostolic pattern was not the only motivation for this orientation. When early Pentecostals encountered God in the power of His Spirit, they wanted to share this experience. For them, Spirit baptism was not a checkbox on the bucket list of experiences they wanted to try. It became the defining experience of their life. Consequently they wanted to share this experience.

The movement's founder, Charles Parham, did not stay long in Topeka, Kansas. He and his first converts traveled first in the tri-state area of Kansas, Missouri, and Oklahoma, and then on to Texas. Parham established a base in Houston and from it sent bands of workers throughout southern Texas. They preached on street corners or wherever they could draw a crowd. As soon as a work was established they moved on the next town. They referred to their works not as churches but as missions and their members as workers. This further underscores their missionary nature.

The famous Azusa Street revival in Los Angeles followed the same pattern. While the building at 312 Azusa Street served as the center for revival, groups spread throughout the Los Angeles basin, aggressively spreading the Pentecostal message. In addition to this local outreach, Azusa had visitors from around the world. Soon after these visitors had experienced Spirit baptism they departed from Los Angeles, committed to taking this good news around the world. In recognition of this pattern, Pentecostal historian Vinson Synan has called Los Angeles the American Jerusalem. In addition to physically traveling and preaching the gospel, participants in the Azusa Street mission published a periodical that was widely circulated, which spread the Pentecostal message.

Patterned as it was on the apostolic church in Acts, the new Pentecostal movement had little organizational structure. The Book of Acts gave very little insight into the structure of the church. There were hints of organization in Acts 15 when Barnabas and Paul were called to Jerusalem to explain the happenings at Antioch, but no pattern for organizational structure was outlined. As the modern Pentecostal movement grew it struggled with how much, if any, organization should be developed. However, the desire to be more effective in world missions provided an important catalyst to organize. The passion for missions compelled most Pentecostals to lay aside their reluctance to organize. Contemporary Pentecostal churches have developed wide networks of missionary activities.

Missions is woven into the fabric of Pentecostalism. Spirit-empowered Christians seek to share their faith with their neighbors who live next door and their neighbors who live on the next continent. They are committed to taking the gospel message to the end of the earth. After all this is the mission of Jesus.

Part III

Our Stories

CHAPTER 9

This Is Our Story: A Brief History of Pentecostalism

T he Book of Acts presents a vibrant church—albeit not a perfect church—but nevertheless a vibrant church. Its apostolic leaders not only demonstrated what it means to be Spirit led, they also possessed the clearest insight into the expectation of Jesus regarding His church. Unfortunately the apostolic pattern was soon lost. By the early fourth century the church had moved a great distance from its founding principles. The Pentecostal story is a story about the return to the apostolic roots of the church. In the words of the prophet Isaiah, "For precept must be upon precept, precept upon precept; line upon line, line upon line; here a little, and there a little" (Isaiah 28:10).

The Constantinian Fall of the Church

Although the drift was gradual, nothing illustrates the distance the church had moved better than the insertion of the Roman Emperor Constantine into the life and doctrinal disputes of the church. (History always contains a complex number of influences and what follows in this chapter is a necessary oversimplification of the events and influences. The events and people mentioned are important but they are only representative of more complex interactions.) In AD 325, the Roman Emperor Constantine called the first ecumenical council of the church to settle an ongoing dispute about the deity of Jesus Christ. The exact details of the dispute are extraneous to this discussion; however, the way in which Constantine both called and presided over a church council is the issue. He insisted the bishops come to an agreement and when they were unable to, he essentially chose a position himself and attempted to impose this view on the church. Historians often call this the Constantinian fall of the church. It marks the beginning of Christendom, the merger of the state and the church and this hastened the departure from the apostolic roots of the church.

The Road Home

The institutional church drifted far from the apostolic pattern for the church. In the sixteenth century Martin Luther helped the Christian faith make a turn back towards the apostolic roots of the church. His insistence that the Scripture alone was the rule of faith (***sola scriptura***) caused people to re-examine the apostolic message. Because centuries of tradition had obscured the biblical pattern, it took time to make it back to the beginning. This desire to return to the apostolic beginnings is often called the restoration impulse.

In the eighteenth century John Wesley moved the church closer to the apostolic faith. Wesley is often called the grandfather of the Pentecostal movement due to his insistence that one need to experience Christ. Christ must be encountered—He cannot be known simply by assenting to creeds and rituals. Wesley and George Whitefield were influential in the development of the Great Awakening that helped turn Western Europe and North America toward God.

The last half of the nineteenth century brought three additional restorational influences. The first was known as the Holiness movement, which grew out of Wesley's doctrine of perfection. The Holiness movement increasingly began to refer to this post-conversion experience as the baptism of the Holy Ghost. The second influence was the Keswick or Higher Life movement. Its genesis was in Great Britain, and its emphasis was on the higher Christian life and possession of the Spirit for an enduement of power focused attention on Spirit baptism. The Keswick movement highlighted the need for spiritual power.

The third influence was the divine healing movement. Dr. Charles Cullis of Boston is usually credited as the founder of the American divine healing movement, or—as he would call it—the faith-cure movement. His methodology included homeopathic care and encouragement in faith in the context of a healing home. He had witnessed these homes while in Europe and opened one in Boston. The infirmed were encouraged to come for care and to live in an environment of faith that would, in turn, nurture their faith. The idea of faith homes spread and became an accepted practice in the movement. It was in keeping with this praxis that Charles Parham opened Bethel Healing Home in Topeka, Kansas, in 1898.

The Birth of the Pentecostal Movement

Charles Parham was a Holiness preacher based in Kansas who was searching for a further restoration of truth beyond just divine healing. He visited a number of sites around North America that he felt were moving closer to what God desired for the church. In 1900 Parham had established Bethel Bible College in Topeka, Kansas. He appeared to model his school on one he had recently visited in Maine. Frank Sanford had founded this school, which he called the Holy Ghost and Us School. Like Sanford, Parham was the primary teacher and the Bible was the only textbook.

As the century closed out, Parham challenged his students to determine if the Book of Acts revealed if there was a uniform evidence of the reception of the Spirit, and if so, what it was. Parham then left for a trip and when he returned he asked his students if they had found any answers for his questions. They replied that the Book of Acts demonstrated that speaking in tongues appeared to be the uniform evidence of Spirit baptism.

On New Year's Eve of that year the college gathered for a Watch Night service. Agnes Ozman asked Parham to lay hands on her so that she might receive the Spirit. He consented and Ozman began to speak in other tongues, reportedly Chinese. Soon other students and Parham himself had received the experience. Parham taught that the full gospel included three distinct works of grace: salvation, sanctification, and the baptism of the Holy Spirit. Given the restorationist nature of the movement, Parham called his work the Apostolic Faith Movement. Historians often refer to the events of Topeka as the birth of the modern Pentecostal movement.

The new movement had difficulty in gaining traction in the Topeka area and for a couple of years made little progress. However, in 1903 a breakthrough occurred in the mining town of Galena, Kansas. Hundreds were filled with the Holy Ghost and the movement began to spread in the tri-state region of Kansas, Missouri, and Oklahoma. Before long Parham visited Texas and Houston became a center for the revival.

As was his custom, Parham opened a Bible school in Houston. William Seymour, an African-American Holiness preacher, was one of the students in the school. Seymour had been introduced to Parham by Lucy Farrow, a pastor of an African-American Holiness church in Houston who had connections with Parham. Seymour would be instrumental in taking the movement to a new level.

The Azusa Street Revival

In February 1906 Seymour received an invitation, on the recommendation of Neely Terry who had heard him preach in Houston, to become the pastor of a small Holiness mission in Los Angeles. The mission, located on the corner of Ninth and Santa Fe, had been founded by Julia Hutchins, who now wanted to go to Liberia as a missionary and was looking for a successor. Parham resisted Seymour's call to Los Angeles for a number of reasons—one of the primary reasons was because Seymour had not yet received the baptism of the Holy Ghost—but he reluctantly accepted his student's decision to go.

When Seymour arrived in Los Angeles things did not work out as he had anticipated at the Ninth and Santa Fe mission. The leadership of the congregation rejected his Pentecostal message and the new minister was forced to abandon his charge. A family in the congregation, Edward and Mattie Lee, invited Seymour to temporarily stay with them. He and the Lees frequently prayed together and soon their prayer meetings grew. Frank Bartleman, who would be instrumental in publicizing the Azusa Street revival, visited the prayer meetings in the Lee home. The meetings outgrew the Lee home and moved to Richard and Ruth Asberry's home located at 214 Bonnie Brae Street. On April 6 Lucy Farrow, who had come to Los Angeles at Seymour's request, laid hands on Edward Lee and he received the baptism of the Holy Ghost. That evening revival broke out in the Asberry home. Seymour received his baptism in the Spirit on April 12. The crowds soon outgrew the Asberry home and Seymour secured a vacant AME church building located at 312 Azusa Street for his growing congregation. The rest, as they say, is history.

The Azusa Street mission became the cradle of Pentecostalism. The events that transpired over the next three years transformed the Apostolic Faith movement into a worldwide phenomenon that changed the face of Christianity. Not only did hundreds of people receive the baptism of the Holy Ghost, but also the message of Pentecostalism also rapidly spread across North America and around the world.

Seymour called his mission the "Pacific Apostolic Faith Mission" and his periodical *The Apostolic Faith*. The reports published in this paper and in contemporary Holiness periodicals, primarily written by Frank Bartleman, drew people to Azusa Street. Most were baptized in the Spirit and committed to this new movement.

A number of missions in the Los Angeles basin were open to Azusa's fire. Workers followed the streetcar lines to cities like Pasadena and Whittier and new works sprang up. But the impact of Azusa was felt far beyond Los Angeles. Glenn Cook laid aside his administrative duties at the mission and embarked on an evangelistic trip to the heartland of America. In St. Louis, Indianapolis, and Memphis he found receptive audiences. As word of the revival spread, both the curious and the seekers made their way to the Azusa mission. For example Charles H. Mason of the Church of God in Christ arrived from Memphis, Tennessee, with questions about the happenings at Azusa. He left Spirit-baptized and, though not without struggle, transformed the Church of God in Christ into a Pentecostal organization. G. B. Cashwell from Dunn, North Carolina, crossed the continent to see the revival firsthand. He was initially appalled that it was led by a black man, but his spiritual hunger overcame his racial prejudice and he received the baptism of the Holy Spirit when Seymour laid hands on him. Cashwell returned to Dunn and was instrumental in the Pentecostal Holiness Church and the Church of God, Cleveland, Tennessee, accepting the Azusa message. The Azusa fire spread north to Portland, east to Chicago, and to the Canadian cities of Winnipeg and Toronto. Missionaries left Azusa empowered by the baptism of the Spirit and circled the globe.

The fledgling Pentecostal movement not only experienced explosive growth as a result of the Azusa Street revival, but it was also indelibly changed by the revival. Pentecostalism, at least for a short time, became consciously interracial and multi-ethnic. As Frank Bartleman famously said, "The color line was washed away in the blood." Blacks, whites, and Latinos worshiped together, and in the narrative that became constructed around Azusa, this both witnessed the power of God and evoked a hunger to replicate the revival. A distinctive Pentecostal worship was birthed at Azusa, perhaps influenced by its African-American founders.

The Finished Work Message

The North Avenue Mission in Chicago, led by William Durham, became a vibrant center of Pentecostalism. Durham became convinced that the Book of Acts did not teach three distinct works of grace. In particular, he was convinced that the Bible did not teach that sanctification was a distinct work of grace. Rather, sanctification began at salvation and was an ongoing work in the life of a believer. He first presented his ideas in a message he called "The Finished Work of Calvary." A large segment of the Pentecostal movement embraced Durham's teaching as another step in the restoration of apostolic truth. The new message brought the first fissure to the new movement. Unfortunately Durham died before he could explore the next step in the restoration of truth.

The New Issue

In the months that followed Durham's death, Finished Work advocates sought to restore a measure of unity within the Pentecostal movement. One venue used to accomplish this was the World-Wide Apostolic Faith Camp Meeting, which was held in Arroyo Seco, California, beginning in April 1913.

The primary organizer for the camp meeting, R. J. Scott, had been instrumental in a previous camp meeting at the same location back in 1907. Tents were pitched for a half mile under the sycamore trees. Scott felt that God had instructed him to organize the camp so that, as the Pentecostal revival expanded, there would be room for the growing crowds. The crowds did arrive from Azusa and the surrounding missions and Scott felt that he had indeed heard from the Lord.

During the late fall of 1912, R. J. Scott visited Maria Woodworth-Etter's enormously successful revival campaign in Dallas, Texas. Crowds as large as five thousand visited her meetings nightly and many more were turned away. In addition to the many miracles witnessed during the campaign, she urged her hearers to be ready for the soon return of Jesus. Her push for unity particularly impressed Scott and he felt that God was leading him to organize a camp meeting similar to the one he had helped develop during the Azusa glory days. He shared this burden with Woodworth-Etter and, as a result, she agreed to lead a month-long camp meeting in the spring of 1913.

People came to Arroyo Seco by the thousands and the meeting originally scheduled to last a month stretched to six weeks. Hundreds were healed and baptized with the Spirit. Nonetheless, a number of preachers resisted turning the meeting completely over to Woodworth-Etter. They wanted to hear from a variety of preachers and, when one speaker preached from Jeremiah 31:22 about God doing a "new thing," a heightened sense of expectation filled the campgrounds.

R. J. Scott asked R. E. McAlister, a Canadian evangelist to preach a baptismal service held at the camp. McAlister decided to take the opportunity to speak on his developing understanding of the proper biblical baptismal formula. He noted that some practiced a "trine immersionist method," baptizing the candidate three times in order to honor each person of the Godhead. He rejected this practice and insisted that the apostles baptized their converts only once and that in Jesus' name.

This settled the crowd and the baptismal service continued. However, John Schaepe, who had spent the night in prayer, felt that God had revealed to him the oneness of God and baptism in Jesus' name. The next day he ran through the camp proclaiming his new revelation. In the following months, God began to deal with Frank Ewart, G.T. Haywood, and Glenn Cook about these ideas. It was almost a year later that Ewart and Glenn Cook baptized each other in Jesus' name and the New Issue was launched. It was called the New Issue in reference to the first issue, which was the Finished Work message.

The events that occurred in the aftermath of the Arroyo Seco camp meeting are important to understand the development of Pentecostalism for a number of reasons. Rebaptism seemed to be a point of contention because it called into question the efficacy of Trinitarian baptism. In the incubation period that occurred in Los Angeles, Jesus Name baptism became the catalyst for a new understanding of both the Godhead and the new birth. Like much of Pentecostalism, these ideas did not appear suddenly. Rather, a number of influences factored into their development, but the timeframe immediately after Arroyo Seco saw these ideas blossom into a new flower.

The Pentecostal church had returned to its apostolic roots. Like Peter, Pentecostals understood that Acts 2:38 best explained the process of salvation. Just like the Book of Acts church, it quickly began to grow. Soon the Spirit was being poured out around the globe. By the end of the twentieth century it had blossomed into the most significant revival movement in the history of Christianity. It had grown from a movement on the margins of society to the most vibrant force within the Christian faith. Pentecostal worship, once maligned as "holy-roller" religion, had transformed most faith traditions.

For Further Study

Foster, Fred J., *Their Story: 20th Century Pentecostals*. Hazelwood, MO: Word Aflame Press, 1965, 1983.

Clanton, Arthur and Charles Clanton. *United We Stand*. Hazelwood, MO: Word Aflame Press, 1995.

As Many as the Lord Our God Shall Call

Pentecostals are diverse. Although they come from many backgrounds, initially most came from the margins of society. They illustrate the old Sunday school song, "red and yellow, black and white, they are precious in His sight." The roots of modern Pentecostalism grew in North American soil, however from its earliest days it has always been a worldwide phenomenon. This final chapter includes the stories of six Pentecostals who are representative of the wider movement. They are stories of healing, deliverance, and Spirit baptism. They tell of people who are eager to embrace Pentecostalism and those who were hesitant in their embrace.

Mary Arthur's Pentecostal story begins shortly after the birth of the movement. Eucaris Agudelo, a young Colombian convert, helped spark the outbreak of Pentecostalism in South America in the mid-twentieth century.

Gary Biggar's story illustrates the transforming power of the Holy Spirit. He was delivered from alcoholism and became a Pentecostal preacher. Arash Ahmadpour is an Iranian immigrant who became a Pentecostal in the United States. Margaret Ronia grew up struggling to understand what it meant to be a Pentecostal in India. Disillusioned with the faith of his childhood church, Chris Anderson embarked on a quest to find truth and meaning in life. He attempted to cobble together pieces from a wide array of religious practices but ended up using alcohol and drugs to medicate the spiritual void in his life. An encounter with the power of the Holy Spirit changed his life.

Mary Arthur

Mary Arthur's journey into Pentecostalism came as a result of a number of significant health issues that impacted her ability to live a productive life. She suffered with chronic digestive troubles as well as issues with her sight. Not only did she have difficulty seeing but she also experienced chronic pain associated with her eye disease. Mary had exhausted the medical help available at the beginning of the twentieth century. Additionally she tried a number of alternative remedies without success. In 1903 her husband, a business owner in Galena, Kansas, insisted she visit Eldorado Springs, Missouri, to see if the hot springs located there could bring relief for her suffering.

Shortly after her arrival in Eldorado Springs, Mary heard the itinerant Kansas evangelist Charles Parham preach in a park near the springs. Parham invited those seeking salvation or healing to a cottage meeting. Arthur responded to the invitation. She had read in James that if elders laid hands on those who were sick, they could be healed. (See James 5:14-15.) She was prayed for and her sight was restored and the chronic pain she had experienced ceased. She was ecstatic with the change in her health

Arthur, who had been a longtime member of Galena's Methodist Episcopal Church, invited Parham to Galena to preach the Apostolic Faith message. He accepted her invitation and within months a significant Pentecostal revival broke out in Galena. Hundreds experienced the power of the Holy Spirit. Like many revivals the Galena revival lasted less than a year. However, out of it grew a Pentecostal church, which Mary Arthur served as pastor for a number of years.

Eucaris Agudelo

Like many from the mountain village of La Morena, seventeen-year-old Eucaris Agudelo relocated to Cali, Colombia, in search of a better life. While in Cali she was invited to a new church in the Cali barrio of La Britania organized by Missionary Bill Drost. In spite of Drost's faulty Spanish, Eucaris grasped enough of his message to seek for the baptism of the Holy Spirit. Soon she received the Spirit and the experience so changed her life that she decided to return to La Morena to share it with her family and friends.

A crowd gathered in her father's house and Eucaris shared how the power of the Holy Ghost had changed her life. The Spirit fell on this group and thirteen people were Spirit baptized. The excitement grew until large crowds gathered nightly and lives began to change.

Saul Ramirez, a cousin of Eucaris, owned and operated the principal cantina in La Morena. It was a gathering place for banditos and others who lived on the edge of the law. Soon the bar was empty of customers and Saul became enraged by the changes happening in his village. One evening he grabbed his pistol and made his way to house where the Pentecostal meeting was being held. When he arrived he pushed his way through the crowd only to find his former customers on their knees crying for mercy from God. He accused Eucaris of evoking this response. She replied that they were feeling the power of God and challenged Saul to see his need of Jesus Christ. Saul fell to his knees and gave his life to God. He went back to his cantina, destroyed all the liquor, and closed the establishment. His conversion impacted the entire community.

Within six months over five hundred converted to Pentecostalism. However, opposition to the new movement also grew. As in the Book of Acts, revival brought persecution, which culminated in a massacre in La Morena. Scores of converts were lined up against a wall and shot. This persecution caused new converts to flee the area and soon Pentecostals from La Morena had migrated throughout Colombia and into the major cities in many South American countries. Among those who migrated were Eucaris and her husband, Nicolas Alveraz, who relocated to Quito, Ecuador, where they pastored a church.

The Eucaris story is a proto-typical Pentecostal story. A young girl, barely on the cusp of womanhood, on the lower end of a socio-economic scale received the baptism of the Holy Spirit, which in turn, empowered her to become the catalyst for a great South American revival.

Arash Ahmadpour

Arash was born in 1985 in Esfane, Iran, during a volatile time in the nation's history. The Shah of Iran had stepped down and a new regime had come into power. Arash's father was an advocate for democracy and an outspoken critic of the new regime. As a result of his advocacy, his father lost his job and was blacklisted from other means of employment. His forced unemployment drove him to his knees to ask God for an answer. He prayed for safe travel to another country where his six children could live in a safer environment. God answered him.

As He often does, God took a tragic event and used it for good. A violent earthquake rocked Tehran and in the confusion and chaos that followed the Ahmadpour family escaped from Iran. They led the authorities to believe they were headed for the airport. The authorities planned to apprehend them when they arrived. At the last moment, Arash's father rerouted the family to the train station and they escaped Iran.

They settled first in Bulgaria and then moved to Turkey. While in Turkey they applied for political asylum in the United States. Their request was granted and the family relocated to Lansing, Michigan. They lived temporarily with their aunt until more permanent housing could be secured. Their aunt's next-door neighbors were Pentecostals and they invited the Ahmadpours to a church service. Arash's father rejected the invitation. Eventually they found a place in East Lansing. One Easter a neighbor invited them to church. They accepted the invitation, not knowing the neighbors were Pentecostals who attended the same church they had rejected earlier. Arash and his family were filled with the Spirit and became members of that local assembly and Arash is currently preparing for ministry.

Margaret Ronia

Margaret was brought up in a Pentecostal home in Kerala, India. As a pastor's daughter in a non-Christian society, she lived a separated lifestyle. However, as she matured she began to realize that she did not share her family's faith. Because of her father's position she felt pressured to pretend to be a Christian, but she did not have a personal experience with God.

While living at a boarding school during her teen years, she experienced a deep sense of loneliness that was exacerbated because of her perceived Christian commitment. In an attempt to gain acceptance she experimented with the religions of her fellow students, however this led to a growing sense of guilt for abandoning her parent's faith. This inner turmoil awakened the first stirring of faith in her heart.

At home, during a summer break from college, she witnessed her mother praying and crying alone in her room. At first she thought her mother was attempting to manipulate her emotions. One day as she listened to her mother pray for strength and companionship, Margaret's heart experienced a change. The next morning she joined her mother in prayer. A sense of love, warmth, and relief washed over her. She became her mother's prayer partner and committed her life to Jesus Christ.

Her new commitment changed the direction of her life. She set aside her career in science and determined to dedicate her life to ministry. A deep burden gripped her heart for the millions of women in India who suffer because of the bondage of false religion. To prepare for this mission she enrolled in a seminary in the United States. During her first semester Margaret received the baptism of the Spirit and this experience deepened her commitment to sharing the gospel and also gave her a sense of empowerment for the mission.

Gary Biggar

Gary Biggar was born in a small village of McAdam, New Brunswick, the youngest of fourteen children to Robert and Jean Biggar. One month after his seventeenth birthday he convinced his mother to sign a waiver allowing him to enlist in the armed forces of Canada. In enlisting in the service he was following a well-worn family path; eight of his brothers had also served in the forces.

In 1961 the military posted him to Germany. It was here that his life began to take a wrong direction. Like many young soldiers, he coped with the stress of military life by drinking and soon the early tentacles of alcoholism began to invade his life.

Gary remained in the armed forces for twelve years. In 1970 while still enlisted in the service he and his wife rented a restaurant on a seasonal basis. The following year they bought a building and renovated it into another restaurant. In 1972 they built a second one; he managed one and his wife the other.

Alcohol increasingly became a crutch to help cope with life and its stresses. Soon the servant became the master. Gary's alcoholism began to take a greater and greater toll on his marriage and family. However, when he was drinking he would think about God.

In 1974 the Biggars returned to McAdam, hoping for a new start in life. They opened a new restaurant but life continued to unravel. In February 1975, Gary was at the end of his rope. One evening he showed up at his restaurant drunk. He told his wife he was going to church. A Pentecostal lady who was working for him asked where he was going to go. When Gary replied that he didn't know, she insisted that the Pentecostal church could help him.

Still under the influence of alcohol, he arrived at the church. It was different that he expected. The worship was exuberant and he began to feel the presence of the Lord. When the pastor asked if there was anyone who wanted to be baptized, a young lady went to the front of the church and Gary followed, although unsure of what was taking place. After prayer by the church elders, Gary was baptized. He emerged from the water, sober and changed. The Biggar family began to attend the Pentecostal church and shortly they were Spirit-baptized. Although the change in their lives was dramatic, it was not without setbacks. However in the next few years Gary matured spiritually. Soon he began to feel a call to ministry. In 1981, the then thirty-eight-year-old family man sold his restaurant and enrolled in Bible college. After assisting in a church he became a pastor. For the next twenty-five years he served as pastor for a number of Pentecostal churches.

Chris Anderson

Through his college years and beyond, Chris Anderson found himself on a perpetual quest for truth. Unimpressed with the faith of his childhood church, he was convinced that Christianity failed to respond to life's most difficult questions. In a quest to find those answers he studied world religions. When something rang of truth, Chris added it to his belief system. As a result, his spirituality reflected a hodgepodge of ideas lifted from Judaism, Buddhism, Hinduism, Egyptian mythology, African spirituality, New Age mysticism, and witchcraft, just to name a few.

Chris used his twenty-something years as an ongoing experiment to bring the unknown into the known. He toured with a heavy-metal band called Joyhammer, whose lyrics challenged Christians and Satanists alike to drop their fairytales and embrace a new, universal spirituality.

After a decade's worth of dabbling with the occult, mixing it with meditation and experimental drug use, Chris's surreal life started to catch up to him. As a chronic marijuana smoker, people started describing him as "burnt out." His search for truth had failed him, and life was feeling meaningless. Slowly, he started to give up, relying on increasing amounts of drugs, alcohol, and pornography to quell his internal strife.

On the brink of despair, once all other spiritual avenues had been seemingly explored and abandoned, God finally sent Chris the answer to his questions. An Apostolic Pentecostal couple, Arvo and Dixie Palm-Leis, challenged Chris with a truth claim. They read Acts 2 with him, stating, "This says that if you believe in Jesus, God will literally manifest Himself to you. This is either a true statement or it's not." This angle dared Chris to reconsider a Christianity he had thrown aside many years earlier.

He entered into Bible study, spending several nights a week and several hours a night exploring God's Word with the Palm-Leis family. Gradually, the things of the Bible came into focus. Chris gave God one month where he would try to follow the Bible's teachings as closely as possible, including curbing his bad habits to the best of his abilities. If God failed to show up in that time, he was determined to move on.

One night, while attending a prayer service at Christ Tabernacle in Herrick, Illinois, Chris felt exhausted at life's trials. Not knowing how else to pray, he collapsed to the floor and said, "I give up, God. I quit. My ways always fail me. I'm giving You complete control." Suddenly he felt a warm rush and a cool breeze, but was convinced that the church was trying to psychologically manipulate him. He waited until he got home and repeated the scene, falling to the floor and giving up. God's presence rushed in again. Through this, Chris realized that God knew his name, and began on a wholehearted quest to receive the Holy Spirit. Later that week, at a revival service in Kentucky, Chris received the baptism of the Holy Spirit. The truth he had been seeking was Jesus Christ all along.

On the Day of Pentecost, Peter reminded his audience that God would pour out His Spirit on all flesh. He promised that the Pentecostal experience was for "all those afar off, even as many as the Lord our God shall call" (Acts 2:39). This promise still holds true today. Around the world and across racial, ethnic, and socio-economic barriers people are embracing Pentecostalism. Or perhaps it would be more accurate to say that people are encountering the power of the Holy Spirit.

For Further Study

Johnston, Robin. *Howard A. Goss: A Pentecostal Life.* Hazelwood, MO: WAP Academic Press, 2010.